Philip Hewitt

Mein Erfolgstrainer
Englische Grammatik

Englisch 9/10

W0338364

Klett Lerntraining

Bibliografische Information der Deutschen Bibliothek
Die Deutsche Bibliothek verzeichnet diese Publikation in der Deutschen Nationalbibliografie; detaillierte bibliografische Daten sind im Internet über http://dnb.ddb.de abrufbar.

Auflage 5. 4. 3. 2. | 2013 2012 2011 2010
Die letzten Zahlen bezeichnen jeweils die Auflage und das Jahr des Druckes.
Das Werk und seine Teile sind urheberrechtlich geschützt. Jede Nutzung in anderen als den gesetzlich zugelassenen Fällen bedarf der vorherigen schriftlichen Einwilligung des Verlages. Hinweis zu § 52a UrhG: Weder das Werk noch seine Teile dürfen ohne eine solche Einwilligung eingescannt und in ein Netzwerk eingestellt werden. Dies gilt auch für Intranets von Schulen und sonstigen Bildungseinrichtungen.
Fotomechanische Wiedergabe nur mit Genehmigung des Verlages.
© Klett Lerntraining GmbH, Stuttgart 2008
Alle Rechte vorbehalten.
Internetadresse: www.klett.de
Zeichnungen: Christa Janik, Leinfelden-Echterdingen: S. 34, 43, 55, 62, 71, 82, 90, 109, 128, 129; Lars Benecke, Hannover: S. 75, 115.
Bildnachweis: S. 54: The Tower of London, istockphoto, Deejpilot, Catgary, Alberta.
Umschlaggestaltung: know idea GmbH, Freiburg, mit Franziska Döhler
Satz: Klaus Bauer, Bondorf
Reproduktion: Meyle + Müller, Medien-Management, Pforzheim
Druck: Medienhaus Plump, Rheinbreitbach
Printed in Germany
ISBN-13: 978-3-12-927138-4

9 783129 271384

Inhalt

Hallo liebe Schülerin, hallo lieber Schüler!

Dein Erfolgstrainer ist genau das richtige Buch für dich,
- wenn du dich in **einem bestimmten Thema verbessern** möchtest
- wenn du dazu **Regeln, Übungen und ausführliche Lösungen** in einem einzigen Buch suchst und
- wenn du wissen willst, wie du **deinen Lernstoff zeitlich am besten einteilst**.

So erstellst du dir dein persönliches Aktiv-Lernprogramm!

Im Inhaltsverzeichnis stehen links alle Themen, die behandelt werden. Rechts werden die Themen zeitlich eingeteilt, damit du dir **dein ganz persönliches Lernprogramm** zusammenstellen kannst und dann sofort siehst, wie viel Stoff du in welcher Zeit erarbeiten kannst.

Lerneinheit: Eine Lerneinheit beträgt 30 – 40 Minuten. Das bedeutet, dass du die Übungen in dieser Zeit schaffen kannst. Aber: Das ist nur ein Richtwert. Wenn du am Anfang länger brauchst – auch kein Problem!
Eine Lerneinheit solltest du an einem Stück bearbeiten. Wenn du 2 (und mehr) Lerneinheiten machen möchtest, ist es jedoch besser, eine 10-minütige Pause dazwischen zu schieben.

Tag: Wie du im Inhaltsverzeichnis siehst, verteilen sich zusammenhängende Themen manchmal auf mehrere Tage. Versuche, an einem Thema dranzubleiben. Wenn du z. B. montags anfängst, bearbeite dienstags die nächste Lerneinheit! So bleibt am meisten hängen und du musst nicht noch mal von vorne beginnen.

Woche/Monat: Wir haben den Lernstoff zusätzlich in Wochen und Monate eingeteilt, damit du sehen kannst, wie viel Zeit du insgesamt für größere Kapitel benötigst.

So hast du immer den Überblick und bist auf den Punkt genau vorbereitet.

Wir wünschen dir viel Erfolg.

P.S. Mit deinem persönlichen Aktiv-Lernprogramm kannst du dich ohne Stress auf deine **nächsten Klassenarbeiten und Tests** vorbereiten.

1 Adjektiv und Adverb

This music sounds **wonderful**. She really plays the saxophone **wonderfully**.

Warum steht im ersten Satz ein Adjektiv *(wonderful)* und im zweiten ein Adverb *(wonderfully)*? Diese und weitere wichtige Fragen im Zusammenhang mit Adjektiv und Adverb werden wir in diesem Kapitel wiederholen.

1.1 Die Unterschiede zwischen Adjektiv und Adverb

Adjektive beschreiben Substantive. Sie stehen entweder:

1. direkt vor dem Substantiv:
   She drives a **fast** car.
2. als Ergänzung hauptsächlich nach *to be, to get, to become* :
   He is **silly**.
   Our teacher got **angry**.

Adjektive werden auch mit *the* benutzt, um bestimmte Gruppen (vor allem von Personen) zu bezeichnen:

The **poor** get poorer and the **rich** get richer.
We are collecting money for the **blind**.

Adverbien (meist Adjektiv + *-ly*) beschreiben:

1. Verben:
   She drives **badly**.
2. Adjektive:
   She is **extremely** clever.
   We were **very** angry.
3. andere Adverbien:
   She speaks **terribly** quickly.

Einige wichtige Adverbien haben Formen ohne *-ly*:

1. Adverbien, die Adjektive oder andere Adverbien beschreiben:
   very, too, far, much
   It's **very** expensive.
2. Einige andere Adverbien, z.B.
   hard, long, high, low, deep, fast

Von Adjektiven, die bereits mit *-ly* enden, wird eine Umschreibung benutzt:

A friendly person smiles **in a friendly way**.

1

a) Read the following passage and list the adverbs used in the three categories given in the rules *„Die Unterschiede zwischen Adjektiv und Adverb"*.

b) Then list all the adjectives used.

The last frontier

Sometime next year, if all goes well, a revolutionary new submarine will be lowered gently into the waters of Monterey Bay for its first voyage. Deep Flight I is shaped like a torpedo but flies faster than other deep-sea research vessels. The pilot, who lies inside the vessel with his or her head in the glass nose, can move as fast as the fastest whale or even leap vertically out of the sea.

More than 100 expeditions have reached the top of Everest, the world's highest mountain, and manned voyages into space have become common. But it is only now that the deepest parts of the ocean are gradually being explored. Sylvia Earle, a co-founder of the company which built Deep Flight I, said, "We know much more about Mars than we know about the ocean floor."

Although scientists are most interested in exploring the deepest parts of the ocean, little is known about the middle waters five to six kilometres down, or even the "shallows" just 100 metres below the surface of the sea.

The oceans are the world's last great frontier. They easily contain more life by weight than any other ecosystem, and their economic potential is equally great. Majestically moving ocean currents influence much of the world's weather. If we can find out how they operate, we could save billions of dollars in weather-related disasters.

The seas contain many valuable minerals and other substances. "The discoveries helpful to mankind will far outweigh those of the space program," says Bruce Robinson of the Monterey Bay Aquarium Research Institute, California. "If we can get to the bottom of the sea fairly regularly, mankind will benefit immediately."

2

When you have checked your answers to exercise 1, put the right forms of the words in brackets into the following sentences.

1. **(careful)** In 1960 the deep-sea submarine *Trieste* was carfully lowered to a depth of 10,912 metres.
2. **(brave)** On board the *Trieste* were two brave scientists.
3. **(good)** The deep-sea submarine behaved well.
4. **(complicated/only)** Unlike the complicated vehicles used today, the *Trieste* contained only the passengers.
5. **(slow/very)** They went down very slowly.
6. **(safe)** They reached the bottom safely.
7. **(soon)** They knew that men would soon be able to explore the depths of the oceans.
8. **(dramatic)** After the *Trieste's* dive, the number of deep-sea submarines increased dramaticly.
9. **(old)** The old American three-person submarine *Alvin*, launched in 1964, is still operating.
10. **(remote/quick)** The first ROVs, vehicles remotely operated from the surface, followed quickly.
11. **(expensive)** These were equipped with expensive cameras and collecting equipment.
12. **(scientific)** Some were built for the army, but others were designed for scientific research.
13. **(marine)** At last marine biologists could collect samples.

14. **(complete)** A completely new era of scientific research began.

15. **(imperfect)** Until then, geologists only had an imperfectly basic knowledge of the seabed.

16. **(endless)** They know now that the sea-floor is not an endless, flat plain stretching from continent to continent.

17. **(close)** Rocks from the sea-bed, when closely examined, were found to contain valuable minerals.

18. **(deep/astonishing)** The new deep-sea submarines can really dive deep astonishing !

3

Here is an unusual crossword puzzle. Follow the arrows to finish the sentences. Use adjectives or adverbs as required. Here are some but not all the words you need. You will have to guess the others from the context:

useful *awful* *first* *unhappy* *full* *loud* *well*

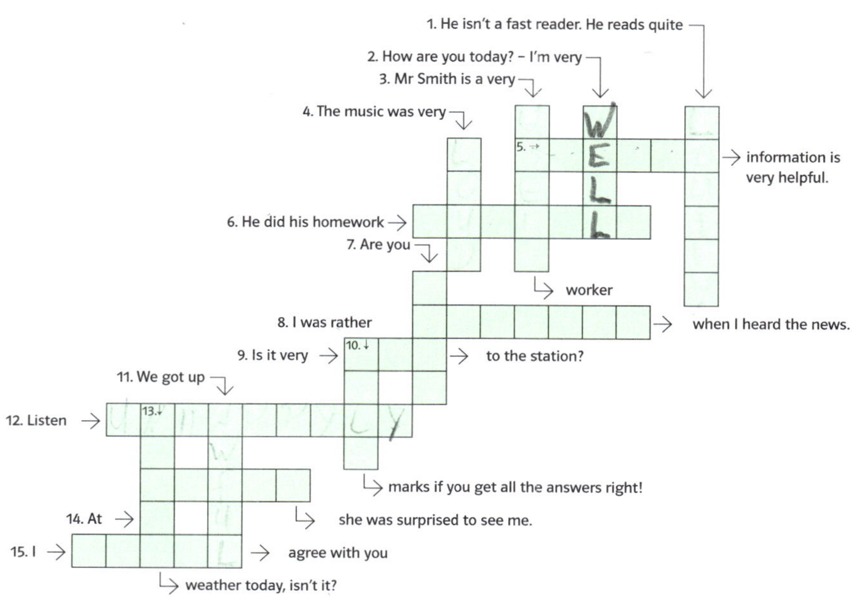

1.2 Die Steigerung von Adjektiven und Adverbien

Adjektive

Einsilbige **Adjektive** werden mit den Endungen *-er, -est* gesteigert:
This car is old**er** than ours.
It's the old**est** car in the street.

Nach kurzem Vokal wird ein einzelner Konsonant verdoppelt:
It's a big house – bi**gg**er than I thought!
End-*e* verschmilzt mit der Endung; *-y* wird zu *-i* vor der Endung:
1995 was the fin**e**st and dr**ie**st summer in Britain for 300 years.

Zweisilbige Adjektive mit sehr kurzer zweiter Silbe (*-y, -ow, -le, -er*) nehmen auch die Endungen *-er, -est:*
We're happ**ier** now.
He is clever**er** than me.

Alle anderen zwei- und mehrsilbigen Adjektive werden durch Anfügung von *more* und *(the) most* gesteigert:
This car is **more** modern and **more** comfortable than your old one.
I think it's the **most** modern and **most** comfortable car I've ever travelled in.

Adverbien

Einsilbige **Adverbien** werden mit den Endungen *-er, -est* gesteigert:
She runs fast**er** than me.
John works quick**er**.

Es gelten die gleichen Rechtschreibregeln wie für Adjektive:
We arrived lat**er** than Melanie.
Peter arrived lat**est/last** of all, as usual!

Die meisten Adverbien werden mit der Endung -ly vom Adjektiv gebildet und haben deshalb zwei Silben. Sie werden mit more und (the) most gesteigert:
You must drive **more** careful**ly**.
Of all the drivers I know, she drives **the most** careful**ly**.

Eine „negative" Steigerung kann man mit *less* und *least* ausdrücken:
This book is **less** interesting than the last one I read.
She worked **less** hard last term.

Unregelmäßige Steigerungen von Adjektiven und Adverbien:

good – better – best	well – better – best
bad – worse – worst	much – more – most
many/much – more – most	badly – worse – worst
little – less – least	little – less – least

4

Put the right form of the word in brackets into the following sentences.

1. **(good)** "Do you know a … fast-food snack-bar? A place where they cook really …?" – "Have you tried McDouglas's? It's … than McSweeny's. I think it's the … place in town."
2. **(bad)** "Well, it can't be … than McDougall's. My sister Sue says they make the … salads in London." – "How is your sister Sue?" – "She's not doing … . She's got a new job.
3. **(interesting)** She says it's much … than her old one." –
4. **(happy)** "I thought she was … at her old job." – "Well, she's … at this new job. She says the people who work there are the … people she's ever worked with. By the way, how are you getting on at school?" – "I'm not very … about my progress ."
5. **(difficult)** "You're learning Italian now, aren't you? Do you find it … than French?" – "No, it's … than French. I think French is the … language I have ever tried to learn!"
6. **(much)** "I don't have … time for sports now. I had … time last year. I don't have as … money for my hobbies either." – "You have too … hobbies! You should arrange your time … carefully."
7. **(little)** "Most parents have … time for talking to their children than for watching TV." – "I don't know about that. My mother is so busy that she only has a … time for TV. She watches TV … than my father. I think she watches the … TV of all of us!"
8. **(good/bad)** "Do you feel … today?" – "I feel … than I felt yesterday." – "Don't you think it would be … to stay in bed?" – "No. I can work … if I lie on the sofa." – "Work?" – "Yes, I've got exams at school in three weeks! I must do … this year because I did so … last year. They were my … exams ever!" – "You'd … ask the doctor to excuse you. You won't do … in your exams if you're ill. Your results will be … than last year's!"
9. **(extreme)** "I don't like our headmaster. He has … views on education." – "He's … strict, I know. But I don't think he's … than most headmasters." – "Well, he's the … headmaster I've ever met!"

1.3 Die Stellung von Adverbien im Satz

1. **am Satzanfang** stehen:

- Zeitbestimmungen: **On Mondays** we go swimming.
- Ortsbestimmungen, die betont werden: **In London** (not in Birmingham) people speak a dialect called Cockney.
- Einwort-Adverbien, die sich auf den ganzen Satz beziehen: **Unfortunately** we can do nothing to help you.

2. **am Satz- oder Satzteilende** stehen:
- Ortsbestimmungen: On Mondays we go swimming **in the open-air swimming pool**.
- Zeitbestimmungen: We go swimming **on Mondays**.
- Enthält ein Satz zwei Zeitadverbien, steht die genauere Zeitbestimmung meist am Satzende: **Next year** she's visiting New York **in the spring**.
- Orts- und Zeitbestimmungen: Im Gegensatz zum Deutschen steht **ORT vor ZEIT:** We're going **to Leipzig tomorrow evening**. *(vgl.: Wir fahren **morgen Abend nach Leipzig**.)*

3. **vor dem Vollverb** (aber nach einem Hilfsverb und *to be*) stehen:
- Adverbien der Häufigkeit:
  She **often** gives parties.
  I have **never** seen you before!
  We are **always** at home from 5 p.m. onwards.

- Auch andere Adverbien (besonders Zeitadverbien), die sich auf den ganzen Satz beziehen und nicht zu stark betont werden sollen:
  I **suddenly** realized who the girl was.
  We **already** knew the answer. (*knew* wird betont)
  We knew the answer **already**. (*already* wird betont)

4. Adverbien der Art und Weise stehen
- unbetont vor dem Vollverb: The town **quickly** doubled its population.
- meist nach dem Vollverb: She drives **carefully** in towns.
- nach Vollverb + Objekt: He speaks English **excellently**.
- nach Präposition + Objekt: They looked at the picture **carefully**.

5

Stell dir vor, du verbringst einige Tage auf dem Land in England. Du willst natürlich wissen, was man besonders beachten soll, wenn man unterwegs ist. Lies dir die Empfehlungen und Anweisungen des *Country Code* durch und liste dabei die Adverbien auf, die in die Kategorien 1–4 der Regeln „Die Stellung von Adverbien im Satz" fallen.

When you are walking or camping in the country, you should always observe

The Country Code

1. If you are walking in the country: Keep to the paths. You should never walk across fields where crops are growing. Most paths are clearly marked. Follow them carefully and don't take short cuts. Farmers don't usually mind if you walk across a meadow where cows or sheep are grazing. Sometimes there is high grass in a field which a farmer has planted specially. If you thoughtlessly walk across this field, it will be difficult for the farmer to cut the hay later.

2. If you are camping: Always ask permission before you camp in a field. Farmers will not often refuse permission (even though they almost always charge a small sum of money). In the dry summers which we have been having it is very easy to start a field or forest fire. So don't have a barbecue unless you are perfectly sure that your fire is safe. It is probably best to ask the farmer first.

3. If you have a dog with you: Keep your dog under control at all times. Dogs often run after other animals. A strange dog will certainly frighten farm animals and may possibly injure them. Dozens of sheep and lambs are killed on British farms each year – and many dogs are shot by angry farmers because their owners have not kept them properly under control, especially during the lambing season.

LOOK AFTER BRITAIN'S COUNTRYSIDE – IT'S THE ONLY ONE WE HAVE!

1. Adverbien bzw. adverbiale Bestimmungen am Satzanfang: …
2. Adverbien bzw. adverbiale Bestimmungen am Satz- oder Satzteilende: …
3. Adverbien vor dem Vollverb (ohne Adverbien der Art und Weise): …
4. Adverbien der Art und Weise: …

Alle gefunden? Super! Probleme bei einer bestimmten Art von Adverbien? Dann schau dir die Beispielsätze auf der linken Seite nochmals an.

6

Put the parts of these sentences in the right order.

1. at ten o'clock / we / to bed / go / often
2. they / in London / have / lived / always
3. to Spain / next year / we / are / flying / in the autumn
4. his car / was / driving / fast / not / very / he / luckily
5. never / she / in December / has / been / to London
6. I / TV / watch / at the weekends / rarely
7. she / looked at it / once / closely / only
8. nearly / yesterday / he / drove / into a wall / his new motor scooter
9. we / eat / in summer / salad / for lunch / regularly
10. do you / come / often / on Fridays / to the youth club?

7

Put the words in these sentences in the right order. You will have to decide which of the words should be adverbs, and add the "-ly" ending, if necessary.

1. when we arrived at the campsite / it / late / was / terrible
2. we / at this site / had / stayed / often / before / but / so that was no problem
3. our tent / we put up / quick / unbelievable / and / in our sleeping bags / were / afterwards / soon
4. up / later / about an hour / woke / I
5. someone / quiet / I could hear / walking around the campsite
6. loud / my friend Tom was snoring / beside me
7. he / a / sleeper / heavy / was
8. last / perhaps the warden was / making a / check / quick / before going to his own bed / happy
9. I / quiet / heard / very / voices / then
10. soft / were talking /a man and a woman / to each other
11. "impossible / this is / a(n) / place / absolute / !" said the man
12. "here / we / possible / can't / put up our tent / in the middle of the night. People are trying to sleep!"
13. "If we / early / and arrived / had left / before midnight / here / everything would have been OK.
14. Now we'll have to / get up / and ask the warden / early / if we can stay. It's all your fault."
15. "Why / my fault / always / is it / ?" asked the man. "You're the one / keen / who is / terrible / so / on camping / !"

16. "Be / quiet / !" whispered the woman. "someone up / You'll wake / ."
17. they didn't know / already / that they had / woken me up

8

Look at the pictures and tell the story. Use the adjective and adverb forms of the words above the pictures. Use both forms if you can make sensible sentences with them! Start like this:

A day in the country

The weather was very ... when we arrived in the Scottish Highlands. The sun was shining ...

1.4 Adjektiv oder Adverb?

Nach Verben, die Zustände (to be) oder Zustandsänderungen *(to get, to become)* ausdrücken, steht die Adjektivform, nicht die Adverbform. Grund: Das nach dem Verb folgende Wort beschreibt das Subjekt, nicht das Verb.

Adjektiv	**Adverb**
Subjekt wird beschrieben:	Verb/Handlung wird beschrieben:
She was **happy** to see me. **I** got **angry** with him.	She **smiled** happi**ly**. I began to **shout** angri**ly**.

Auch bei einigen wenigen Verben der sinnlichen Wahrnehmung *(look* = aussehen, *taste, smell, sound, feel*) bezieht sich das hinter dem Verb stehende Wort (wie ein Adjektiv) auf das Subjekt:

Adjektiv:	Adverb der Art und Weise:
That food looks **good**. = **That** food is **good**.	He **looked carefully** at the food.
This cake tastes **nice**.	If you **ask** me **nicely**, I'll give you some.
The meat smells **bad**.	I can't **smell properly** because I've got a cold.
It feels **very cold**. - That's because it's been in the fridge.	He **felt** his way **carefully** through the dark room to the door.
That music sounds **wonderful**.	She **plays** the piano **wonderfully**.

9

Make sentences from this switchboard, but be careful to use the right form – adjective or adverb.

1. The CD 2. We 3. She 4. The explorers 5. Jackie 6. My teacher 7. The food 8. The butler 9. Her singing 10. I	smelt looked felt criticized tasted gave screamed sounded	me their way a the dinner gong	careful/ly unusual/ly angry/angrily terribl(e)/ly delicious/ly beautiful/ly loud/loudly	at the picture. along the tunnel. scream. when he/she saw my homework. after my flight.

10

A vocabulary exercise to finish off with. Sometimes we combine an adverb and an adjective to make one adjective, like this:

A river which flows fast is a *fast-flowing* river.
A boy who behaves badly is a *badly-behaved* boy.

Do the same with the following definitions:

1. An aircraft which flies high is a ______________________.
2. A girl who dresses well is a ______________________.
3. A battery which lasts a long time is a ______________________.
4. A rock concert that has been organized well is a ______________________.
5. A lesson which has not been prepared well is a ______________________.
6. A rose which smells sweet is a ______________________.
7. A girl who looks attractive is an ______________________.
8. A vehicle which moves fast is a ______________________.
9. An old LP which has been scratched badly is a ______________________.
10. Ground which lies low is ______________________.

Adjektiv und Adverb

Unterschiede zwischen Adjektiv und Adverb:

Ein **Adjektiv** kann ein Substantiv beschreiben:
He drives a **slow** car.

Ein Adjektiv ergänzt **anstelle eines Adverbs** Verben, die keine Handlung, sondern einen Zustand ausdrücken (*to be, to become, to get*):
He is **slow**. She got **angry**.

Verben der Wahrnehmung, wo das Subjekt die Handlung nicht ausführt (*to look, to feel, to taste, to smell, to sound*):
It looks **good**. It tastes **good**, too!

Ein **Adverb** beschreibt:

– die Handlung eines Verbs:	He drives **slowly**.
– ein Adjektiv:	He drives an **extremely slow** car.
– ein weiteres Adverb:	He drives **extremely slowly**.

Achtung! Es gibt viele **Adjektive** mit der Endung *-ly*: *friendly, silly, holy, jolly, lowly* (bescheiden). Es gibt aber auch viele wichtige **Adverbien**, die nicht die typische Endung *-ly* haben: *very, too, much, so, high, low, fast, hard, long* etc.

Steigerung von Adjektiven und Adverbien:

Einsilbige Wörter:		
	-er, -est:	He has a **faster** car so he drives **faster** than me.
Zweite Silbe nur *-y/-ow/-le/-er*:		
	-er, -est:	She is **happier** at her new job.
Zwei und mehr Silben:		
	more, most:	This house is **more modern**. She does her work **most thoroughly** *(gründlichst)*.
	less, least:	They must learn to eat their food **less quickly**.

Unregelmäßige Steigerungen findest du in Kap. 1.2.

Stellung im Satz:

Ein Adjektiv steht vor dem Substantiv, das es beschreibt:
This is a **good** book.

Nach *to be, to get, to become* als Ergänzung:
Our teacher was very **pleased**.

Ein Einzeladverb steht normalerweise **nach** seinem Verb:
My dad works **hard**.

Oder nach Verb + Objekt:
She stopped the car **quickly**.

Adverbien der Häufigkeit stehen dagegen **vor** dem Verb:
We have **never** seen him before.

Viele Zeitadverbien stehen auch vor dem Verb:
I **suddenly** felt cold.

Achtung! Im Gegensatz zum Deutschen:
- Kein Adverb zwischen Verb und direktem Objekt:
  He **opened the letter** quickly.
- Ort vor Zeit:
  They went **there yesterday**.

Die Stellung adverbialer Bestimmungen im englischen Satz hängt sehr davon ab, ob eine Orts-oder Zeitbestimmung besonders betont werden soll oder nicht (s. Kap. 1.3).

Jeweils einer der Sätze in den Satzpaaren enthält einen Fehler. Bloß welcher? Schau dir die Sätze genau an und verbessere den fehlerhaften Satz.

1. a) She is a terrible fast eater.

   ____

   b) She eats terribly quickly.

   ____

2. a) My friend John works more slower than me.

   ____

   b) But his homework is tidier than mine.

   ____

3. a) This book isn't as interesting as I thought it would be.

   ____

   b) That film was less interesting as I thought it would be.

   ____

4. a) I got angry to my feet and walked out of the theatre.

   ____

   b) On Friday the weather became terribly hot.

   ____

5. a) Do you think that Melanie is more clever than her brother?

   ____

   b) No, but I think she works harder.

   ____

6. a) We're going to a party tomorrow evening.

   ____

   b) Enjoy yourselves! I'll see you on Monday at school.

   ____

7. a) Last year I read her first book on holiday.

   ____

   b) Have you read already her next book?

   ____

8. a) She hardly worked for her exams.

   ____

   b) She worked for her exams hard.

   ____

9. a) He can't speak French but he speaks fluently *(fließend)* English.

   ____

   b) I speak good French but my English is bad.

   ____

10. a) Your idea sounds wonderful.

   ____

   b) Your idea looks well on paper, too.

   ____

2 Zeitformen zur Wiedergabe von Gegenwart und Zukunft

Preisfrage: Welcher dieser beiden Sätze ist falsch?

1. We speak German. oder **2. We are speaking German.**

Natürlich ist Satz 2 „grammatisch richtig". Die Reihenfolge aller Bestandteile stimmt: (Subjekt) *We* + (Verb) *are* + *speak* + *ing* + (Objekt) *German*. Nur wird dieser Satz sachlich immer falsch sein. Warum? Diese – und andere Fragen zu den Zeitformen, die Gegenwart und Zukunft ausdrücken – wiederholen wir in diesem Kapitel.

2.1 Der Gebrauch von *simple present* und *present progressive*

Die beiden Präsens-Zeitformen

Das englische *simple present* kann anscheinend für fast alles benutzt werden – nur nicht für das, was gerade in der Gegenwart abläuft! Hierfür brauchst du die *progressive form*. Da es im Deutschen keine Verlaufsformen gibt, werden Extrawörter wie z.B. „zur Zeit", „gerade", „bin dabei" benutzt, die im Englischen nicht nötig sind und meist nicht übersetzt werden.

1. **Einfache Beispiele**

Deutsch	**Englisch** ***simple form***	 ***progressive form***
Spricht er Französisch? (allgemein)	**Does** he **speak** French?	
Spricht sie **gerade** Italienisch?		**Is** she **speaking** Italian?
Wir **wohnen** in Deutschland. Sie **wohnt nicht** hier. (allgemeiner Zustand)	We **live** in Germany. She **doesn't live** here.	

	simple form	***progressive form***
Er **wohnt gerade** in Berlin.		He **is living** in Berlin.
Sie **wohnt nicht** (mehr) hier.		She **isn't living** here now.
Sie **kommen immer** spät an.	They **always** arrive late.	
Er **macht** seine Hausaufgaben **oft** im Bus.	He **often does** his homework on the bus.	
Ich **mache gerade** meine Hausaufgaben. (jetzt)		I'**m doing** my homework.

Das ***simple present*** wird für permanente Zustände und regelmäßig wiederholte Tätigkeiten verwendet.
Signalwörter: *always, often, sometimes, never, rarely, seldom, occasionally, every morning* etc.
Das ***present progressive*** wird für das, was gerade geschieht, verwendet.
Signalwörter: *now, at present, at the moment, just, for the time being* etc.

2. **Kniffligere Beispiele**

Deutsch	**Englisch**
Morgen verlasse ich die Schule. Angabe der Zukunft: Präsens im Deutschen …	**Tomorrow I'm leaving** school. *present progressive* im Englischen!
Er **kommt immer** zu spät an! (… Das ist sehr ärgerlich!)	He**'s always arriving** late! *Always* wird sonst nur mit dem *simple present* benutzt.
Unsere Reise **fängt** am Montag **an**. Dein Zug **fährt** um sieben.	Our trip **starts** on Monday. Your train **leaves** at seven.

(Beide Sätze sind Beispiele der so genannten „Fahrplanzukunft".)

Aber zurück zu unserer Eingangsfrage: Warum ist der Satz *"We are speaking German"* zwar grammatisch richtig, sachlich aber falsch? – Weil es für den Augenblick des Sprechens nicht zutrifft. Fängt man den Satz auf Englisch *("We are speaking …")* an, kann es nur heißen *"We are speaking **English**"*.

1

Which form is correct: a, b, c or d?

1. John and Alison ... German at school.
   a) learn b) are learnt c) is learning d) learns
2. John and Alison ... English, so they can't come out to play.
   a) learn b) are learnt c) are learning d) learns
3. We sometimes ... to pop concerts.
   a) are going b) go c) are gone d) were going
4. What ... for! Let's start!
   a) are we waiting b) we wait c) do we wait d) we do wait
5. "Are you busy tomorrow?" – "Yes. I ... tennis with Roger."
   a) play b) am playing c) will play d) shall play
6. "She ... always ... that loud disco music! I can't stand it!"
   a) is ... playing b) playing c) play d) does ... play

2

Translate these sentences into English.

1. Meine Mutter arbeitet zur Zeit nicht in einem Büro.
2. Oliver und Tanja spielen jede Woche Tennis.
3. Gehst du immer um halb acht in die Schule?
4. Er spielt ständig seine Geige!
5. Jetzt lernen sie Spanisch.
6. Er spricht nicht gut Englisch.
7. Geht sie nie schwimmen?
8. Ich spiele nicht Fußball.
9. Er hört selten Jazz.
10. Nächste Woche gehe ich in ein Rockkonzert.
11. Der letzte Bus fährt um Mitternacht.

3

Take a sheet of paper and list the present tense forms in the following advertisement under the three headings:

Simple Form:	Progressive Form:	Modal Auxiliaries
...	...	...

See Britain this year

If you are planning a holiday with a difference, come to England this year!

The south
The Channel coast, from Kent to Dorset, has some of the finest beaches in Britain. The White Cliffs of Dover stand guard over England's biggest ferry port.You can explore the quiet country lanes in your own car. But please drive carefully and watch out for people who want to explore the countryside on foot or on horseback.

The south-west
Devon and Cornwall lie in the extreme south-west of England. Visit Dartmoor and Exmoor, where ponies still live wild. Come to Plymouth and stay at one of the historic old inns that are waiting to welcome you. Are you thinking of spending longer than a week here? Then you might like to rent one of the holiday flats which are to be found in most of the larger towns. Cornwall possesses many interesting relics of Britain's Industrial Revolution and is still the home of china clay mining.

The Midlands
This is the Heart of England: Shakespeare Country. Every year many thousands of people visit the home of the greatest writer in the English language. Tourists love the mellow stone houses which they find in the Cotswolds. Who could resist places which have names like *Bourtonon-the-Water, Stow-on-the-Wold or Moreton-in-Marsh*? But the charm of the Cotswolds does not end with the historic past. Visitors come from all over Europe to explore the beautiful countryside.

The north
Who says there is nothing to see in the North of England?! Not twenty miles from the centre of Manchester lies some of England's prettiest moorland scenery. Yorkshire, with its lovely Dales and its capital, York, where nearly 2000 years of history are waiting to be discovered. Visit Hadrian's Wall on the old Roman border between England and Scotland. It runs from Carlisle on the west coast to Newcastle on the east and is the biggest single national monument in Britain.

What are you waiting for? Write today for our big, free 64-page brochure *Hello England.*
We are looking forward to seeing you in England next year!
BTA, 23 Baker St, London

Verben, die normalerweise nicht in der Verlaufsform verwendet werden:

to be, to have, modale Hilfsverben *(can, must, may, ought to* etc.):	**Ausnahme:** wenn *to be* oder *to have* anstelle eines anderen Verbs benutzt werden, z.B.: He **is being** very difficult. (= behaving badly) We**'re having** breakfast. (= eating) She **is having** a wonderful time. (= enjoying) I**'m having** a bath/shower. (= taking)

Gefühle, Emotionen (in steigender Gefühlsstärke):

like/love/adore:	He **likes / loves / adores** strawberry ice-cream.
dislike/hate/loathe:	She **dislikes / hates / loathes** parties.
want/wish/desire/need:	I **want / wish / desire / need** to see you.
mind:	**Don't** you **mind** living alone?

Besitzverhältnisse:

belong:	This book **belongs** to me.
owe:	She still **owes** me £25.
own/possess:	They **own** three cars at the moment.

Geistige Aktivitäten (wissen, glauben, denken, vergessen etc.):

agree:	He **doesn't agree** with what they are doing.
believe/think:	I **don't think / believe** you are listening to me.
forget/remember/ recall/recollect:	She **remembers** her childhood very clearly.
know:	**Do** you **know** what he is talking about?
mean/signify:	What **does** this word **mean / signify**?
realize/perceive:	He **realizes** now that he is wrong.
see (= understand):	**Don't** you **see** what I mean?
trust:	I think she **trusts** me now.
understand/appreciate:	I **appreciate** your difficult position.

Einige (aber nicht alle) Verben der sinnlichen Wahrnehmung:

feel *(= sich **an**fühlen)* :	This material **feels** soft and warm.
smell/taste:	The food **smells / tastes** good.
sound:	That music **sounds** very familiar. **Ausnahme:** I wonder how she **feels / is feeling**? *(= **sich** fühlen)*

4

Put the verbs in brackets into the right form – simple or progressive.

1. **(not listen)**	"Kevin! You … to me. Wake up!
2. **(go, we – go)**	We usually … to Spain but this year … to Britain."
3. **(have)**	"We had a phone call from some friends. They … a wonderful time there at the moment.
4. **(have)**	They … two young children." –
5. **(they – stay)**	"Where …?" – "In Cornwall. It's warm down there, even at Easter.
6. **(have)**	Every morning they … breakfast on the balcony.
7. **(take)**	Then they … a walk along the beach.
8. **(drive)**	On Thursday they … to Land's End."
9. **(they – come)**	"When … back?" – "Next weekend."
10. **(you – know)**	"… Sue Hennell?" –
11. **(not think)**	"I … so.
12. **(she – live)**	Where …?" –
13. **(stay)**	"I'm not sure. I think she … with her aunt and uncle for a few weeks." –
14. **(you – mean, always arrive)**	"… the tall girl with red hair who … late for school?" –
15. **(believe, be)**	"Yes, I … she … often late.
16. **(not see)**	That's why I … her often." –
17. **(be, you – like)**	"So why … you so interested in her? … her?" –
18. **(owe, need)**	"Good lord, no! But she … me £5 and I … the money to buy a birthday present for Adrian."

5

Write a letter to a penfriend. Tell him/her all about yourself. The switchboard will help you, but don't put words in the same sentence just because they are in the same line. Write at least eight sentences. Start like this:
Dear Penfriend, My name is … and I live in …

1. At the moment 2. 3. Sometimes 4. Every week 5. 6. On Saturdays 7. 8. During the week	I my family we	often seldom usually never	(am) (is) (are)	go live learn eat drink *etc.*	(…ing)	just now.

2.2 Der Gebrauch des *going to-future* und des *will-future*

1. *going to* + Infinitiv
Die Form *going to* + Infinitiv wird für eine zukünftige Handlung benutzt, die beabsichtigt ist. Eine Zeitangabe ist nicht unbedingt erforderlich.
I'm **going to meet** my friend at the station tomorrow.
He**'s going to** lend me his bicycle.

2. Das *will*-Futur (*will* + Infinitiv) wird so verwendet:
- in *if*-Sätzen:
We **won't come** to your party if you aren't nice to us!
Unless you stop smoking you**'ll** never **lose** your cough.

- als „neutrale" Zukunftsform für Handlungen, die sich ereignen werden:
How old **will** Kristin **be** next year? – Fifteen.
After a dry start, rain **will fall** in some areas.
The film **will be shown** in the village hall.

- als „spontane Reaktion":
The phone's ringing and I'm in the bath! – OK, I**'ll answer** it.
This exercise is very difficult. – We**'ll help** you.
What **shall** we **do**? – Don't worry. I**'ll think** of something."

- für Bitten, die als Frage gestellt werden, sowie für Reaktionen darauf:
Will you **shut** up! – I **won't**! I**'ll shout** and **scream**!
What **will** you **have**? – I**'ll have** a cup of coffee.

- mit Verben, die normalerweise nicht in der Verlaufsform benutzt werden (s. Kapitel 2.1):
I hope you **won't think** I'm being rude.
When **will** we **know** the results of our test?

- nach Verben, die eine Meinung, Annahme usw. über die Zukunft ausdrücken: *assume, believe, expect, hope, know, think* sowie mit den Adverbien *certainly, perhaps, possibly, probably, surely* :
I **hope** you**'ll take** a break after this exercise!
Do you **think** she**'ll mind** if we borrow her bike?
Surely she **won't tell** her friends!

3. *shall* oder *will*?
Die Form *shall* wird fast immer nur in Fragen im Sinne von „Soll ich?", „Wollen/Sollen wir?" benutzt. In Aussagesätzen werden ohnehin beide Formen auf -*'ll* abgekürzt.

Shall I call a taxi? – No, that's OK. **I'll** walk.
When **shall** we **meet** again? – What about Tuesday next?
*(= Wann **sollen/wollen** wir uns wiedersehen?)*
When **will** we **meet** again? – Who knows? Perhaps never.
*(= Wann **werden** wir uns wohl **wiedersehen**?)*

Um die vielfältigen Möglichkeiten richtig auszunutzen, musst du also zwischen der Wettervorhersage *(will)*, einer festen Absicht (*going to* + Infinitiv), einer moralischen Pflicht *(shall we?)* und anderen Nuancierungen der Zukunft unterscheiden lernen – am besten anhand von Situationen.

6

First of all, two ways of reacting to the same situation.

Example:

1. You haven't got much money.
   a) You ask a friend to lend you a few pounds until next week:
   "Will you lend me a few pounds until next week?" (= Bitte)
   b) Your friend agrees but hasn't got much money on him today. He promises to lend you some money tomorrow. The next day he forgets. You remind him:
   "Are you going to lend me that money or not?" (= Absicht)
2. A friend asks you about your trip to London.
   a) Next week? b) Buy me a souvenir? Please!
3. It's a hot day and the window is shut.
   a) You think it would be a good idea to open it – but ask the others first!
   b) Perhaps the noise of traffic might be too loud. Ask the others what they think.
4. You go into a sweet shop with a friend. She buys some sweets – but doesn't offer you one! After a while you say:
   a) Not offer me one? b) You – have a stomach-ache if you eat them all!
5. It is dark. The front doorbell rings, but you know the door is locked and you live on the fourth floor in an old house with no house telephone. Who is going to answer the door?
   a) Nobody moves. At last you stand up and say: "OK, ...!"
   b) You ask your younger brother. "(not – answer the door?)"

7

Now for something a bit more complicated. How would you react in the following situations? You are walking along a lonely country road to school when suddenly you see one car crash into another! What do you think or say?

Example:

a) You turn away and walk on. You don't want to get involved.
You think to yourself: *"I'm not going to get involved."*

b) As you walk away you look around. The road is empty, so you think to yourself: "(I – not stop) I am not going to stop"

c) "(nobody – see me) nobody will see me if I walk away."

d) You stop and listen. There is no sound. No people on the lonely road – no traffic. You think: "(someone – arrive – in a few minutes)
someone will arrive in a few minutes.
(be late for school) I am going to be late for school if I wait any longer!"

e) But you can't walk any further. Perhaps the people are badly injured – dead even. You walk back to the cars. One driver is sitting beside his car with his head in his hands. You ask him: "(I – call a doctor?)"
Shall I'm going to call a doctor.

f) The injured man doesn't say anything at first. You say: "Stay here! (I – call a doctor!) I'm going to call a doctor"

g) He looks up and says: "OK, (I – stay here) I will stay here"

h) You look at the other car. There is a young woman in it. She is unconscious.
You say: "I hope (she – OK) she will be OK"

i) The injured man says: "(Try and get her out?) Will you try and get her out?"

j) You can't open the door on the driver's side. You think it may be best if you do not move the woman: "No, I'll waiting for the police."

k) The injured man asks you to call the police, too: "You will call the police, too?"

l) You say: "Yes, OK, It won't be longer (not be long)!"

You run across a field to a nearby farmhouse.

2.3 Das *future progressive*

Ganz richtig – es gibt auch eine Verlaufsform des *will*-Futurs. Wie bei allen Verlaufsformen drückt *will be ...-ing* eher eine längere Handlung als eine Punkthandlung aus.

Die Verlaufsform der Zukunft bietet sich also speziell für Verben an, die **nicht** Kurzhandlungen beschreiben: *live, work, sit, lie, wait, listen, watch, stay* etc.

Vergleiche:

Next year we **will move** to the USA.
but: Next year we **will be living** in the USA.

Verben, die kurze „Einmalhandlungen" ausdrücken, stehen natürlich immer im einfachen *will*-Futur: *ask, stop, start, see, buy* etc.

We**'ll stay** at a nice hotel. (a promise)
but: We**'ll be staying** here for a week.

I **won't wait** for her much longer! *(mein Entschluss)*
but: **I won't be waiting** outside the cinema. *(ich werde woanders warten)*

Come and see me tomorrow and I**'ll bake** a cake.
(= I'll bake it before you come.)
but: Don't come before two o'clock. I**'ll be baking** a cake.
(= I'll be busy doing something else if you come too early.)

Our train **will arrive** at five o'clock. Don't be late!
(= The train is never late – always on time.)
but: Our train **will be arriving** at about five o'clock.
(= You're not sure about the exact time, or perhaps the train is usually late!)

8

Look at the pictures and say what the people will be doing at two o'clock this afternoon.

1

Sue – travel

2

John – iron

3

Mum

4

Dad – garden

5

Julia

6

the boys

7

our teacher

8

Pat and Jean

9

our cat – have lunch

9

Put the right halves of the sentences together.

1. What will you do
2. What will you be doing
3. Don't hit him or
4. Don't disturb him because
5. Will they be having lunch
6. Will they have lunch
7. If we arrive late
8. When we arrive
9. She'll finish work
10. She'll be finishing work

a) at exactly ten past five.
b) he'll probably be sleeping.
c) we will all have breakfast.
d) about now.
e) this time next week?
f) before we arrive?
g) he'll tell the police!
h) if you can't find the key?
i) they will be having breakfast.
j) when we arrive?

2.4 Das *future perfect*

Das *future perfect* wird für Handlungen verwendet, die in der Zukunft abgeschlossen werden:

> Next year I **will try** to learn Spanish.
> In two years' time I **will have learnt** a lot of Spanish
> because I **will have been learning** it for two years.

Wie immer drückt die einfache Form dieser *future perfect tense* eine Punkthandlung bzw. einen Punktzustand aus – in diesem Beispiel den erreichten Stand des Wissens –, während die *progressive form* den andauernden Spracherwerb betont. Ein weiteres Beispiel:

> Mr Wells **is retiring** next month. –
> How long **will** he **have been** a teacher at your school? –
> He **will have been teaching** English there for 45 years.
> He **will have taught** three generations of pupils!

Es gibt auch einen Unterschied zwischen:

> **Will** you **finish** reading your book when we get back?
> **Will** you **have finished** reading your book when we get back?

Der erste Satz ist eine Bitte: Lies dein Buch zu Ende, wenn wir wieder zu Hause sind. Der zweite Satz ist die Frage, ob du es wohl bis dahin fertig gelesen haben wirst.

10

This is what you are doing now. But how much will you have done in the future? Be careful – sometimes you will need the progressive form!

1. I am learning to ride a motor-scooter *(= Roller)* now, but when I am 19 **(pass my driving test)**.
2. Pat is training to be a bank-clerk. In two years' time **(finish her training)**.
3. We are moving to Bristol next month. When we leave our present house **(live there for 10 years)**.
4. "How long **(you learn English)** when you leave school?"
5. "Where's Mike?" – "He's talking to Sally on the phone." – "How long has he been talking to her?" – "In five minutes he **(talk)** to her for exactly an hour!"
6. "I expect John is waiting at the station already." – "Never mind. We'll be there in half an hour. He **(not wait)** long!"
7. This time next week our English teacher **(mark)** our tests.
8. "I'm saving £10 a week. I'm 16 now, so when I'm 18 I **(save)** for two years.
9. I hope I **(save)** enough to take my driving test."
10. "**(they – arrive)** at the airport yet?" – "I expect so."
11. "In 2015 my mother **(work)** at the same office for 25 years." –
12. "Really? My mother **(finish)** working by then."
13. "Shall we take the new motorway to Edinburgh when we go on holiday this summer?" – "I don't think **(they finish)** building it by then."
14. "Karl's a permanent student. Next term he **(study English)** at university for seven years!"
15. "If we don't hurry up they **(drink)** all the wine before we even arrive at the party!"

Zeitformen zur Wiedergabe von Gegenwart und Zukunft

Simple present oder ***present progressive?***
Das englische ***simple present*** wird verwendet,
- wie im Deutschen, für allgemeine, zeitunabhängige Zustände:
  We **live** in Germany.
- wie im Deutschen, für regelmäßig wiederholte Tätigkeiten:
  She often **arrives** late.
- wie im Deutschen, für die so genannte „Fahrplanzukunft“:
  My plane **leaves** at 8.30.

Fragen und Verneinungen werden mit *to do* gebildet:
When **do** you go swimming? He **doesn't** live here.

Das englische ***present progressive*** hat keine deutsche Entsprechung. Diese Zeitform wird im Gegensatz zum deutschen Präsens verwendet,
1. um das, was gerade im Augenblick passiert, auszudrücken:

We **are watching** TV.	Wir **sehen** gerade fern.
What **is** she **doing**?	Was **macht** sie gerade?

2. um die Zukunft auszudrücken, meist unter Angabe des entsprechenden zukünftigen Zeitpunktes:

When **are** you **leaving**?	Wann **geht** ihr?
She**'s arriving** tomorrow.	Sie **kommt** morgen an.

Verben, die keine „verlaufenden“ Handlungen, sondern Zustände oder Besitzverhältnisse (*to be, to own, to possess, to belong, to owe*), Gefühle und geistige Aktivitäten (*to love, to hate, to agree, to believe, to mean, to realize, to trust* usw.) ausdrücken, werden selten oder nie in der *progressive form* verwendet.

Weitere Möglichkeiten, zukünftige Handlungen auszudrücken:

going to **+ Infinitiv**
Diese Form drückt feste Absichten aus:

I**'m going to buy** a new bike.	Ich **kaufe** mir ein neues Fahrrad. / Ich **werde** mir ein neues Rad kaufen.
Is she **going to come** to the party?	**Kommt** sie auf die Party?

***will* + Infinitiv**

Diese Form wird in fast allen anderen Situationen, die mit der Zukunft zu tun haben, verwendet:

- im Hauptsatz in *if*-Sätzen:
  If you help me, I'**ll help** you. — Wenn du mir hilfst, so **helfe** ich dir.
- als „spontane Reaktion“:
  Will you **phone** him or shall I? — **Rufst** du ihn an oder soll ich?
- als neutrale Zukunftsform:
  He **will be** here at six o'clock. — Er wird um sechs Uhr hier sein.

Weitere Einsatzmöglichkeiten, siehe Kap. 2.2. Für die englischen Konstruktionen *going to* und *will* + Infinitiv wird im Deutschen oft das Präsens benutzt.

Future progressive

Wie alle Verlaufsformen drückt auch das *future progressive* eher eine längere Handlung aus, die in der Zukunft ablaufen wird.

I'**ll be travelling** through France next month.

Je länger die Handlung oder je ungenauer die Zeitangabe, umso wahrscheinlicher wird im Englischen die Verlaufsform des Futurs verwendet. Vergleiche den „spontanen“ Entschluss mit dem „beschreibenden“ Satz:

I'**ll sit** in the garden. — She'**ll be sitting** in the garden.

Setze die passende Zeitform des in Klammern vorgegebenen Verbs ein:

1. (stand) Keep your eyes open for me at the station. I ______________________ near the exit.
2. (study) At present my sister ______________________ English at university.
3. (be) Next year she ______________ in Britain for five years already.
4. (work) My mother ______________________ in an office. She's a secretary.
5. (see) "When ________ I ________ you again?"
6. (do) "__________ you __________ anything on Friday evening?" – "No. Why?" –
7. (give) "I ______________________ a party. Would you like to come?" – "Yes, of course!
8. (invite) __________ you ____________ Jean and Paul?" –
9. (complain) "Yes. They ________ always ____________________ that nobody invites them to parties,
10. (invite) but I always ____________________ them to mine!"

3 Das *past tense:* *Simple* oder *progressive form* ?

Die *simple form* drückt eine oder mehrere Handlungen aus, die in einem abgeschlossenen Zeitraum in der Vergangenheit passierte(n):

We **visited** London last year.
We **visited** London several times last year.

1. Als Kontrast zu einer in der *simple form* stehenden, relativ wichtigen Handlung wird die *progressive form* oft für eine „Hintergrundhandlung" benutzt:
   We **visited** London several times while we **were staying** in Brighton.

2. Das *past progressive* steht selten allein. In solchen Fällen schildert es entweder nur den Hintergrund oder eine langsame Entwicklung (= Verlauf):
   I looked out of the window. It **was** still **raining**.
   It **was getting** light. The birds **were beginning** to sing.

   Vergleiche:
   As soon as it **got** light, the birds **began** to sing.
   Relativ schneller Sonnenaufgang (wie in den Tropen) – plötzlich einsetzender Vogelgesang. Hier könnte auch eine immer wiederkehrende Alltagssituation gemeint sein.

3. Manchmal wird die Gleichzeitigkeit von zwei Handlungen dadurch betont, dass beide in der Verlaufsform stehen. Die Frage erkundigt sich nach dem Verlauf bereits begonnener Handlungen:
   What **were** they **doing** when you arrived?
   Sheila **was cooking** and John **was cutting** the grass.

   Die Frage müsstest du aber anders stellen, wenn du die Reaktion auf die Ankunft des Gastes beschreiben wolltest:
   What **did** they **do** when you arrived?
   Sheila **cooked** lunch and John **cut** the grass.
   Die Antwort betont nicht den gleichzeitigen Verlauf, sondern nur die Tatsache, dass beide Handlungen relativ gleichzeitig anfingen und zu Ende gingen.

4. *was …-ing* (oft mit *going to*-Futur) hat häufig die Bedeutung „wollte“, „hatte vor“. Das Hilfsverb muss stark betont werden:
   She ***was*** **meeting** Patrick this evening, but she has changed her mind.
   They ***were*** **going to call** the fire brigade, but they managed to put the fire out themselves.

Merke

Viele Verben können in beiden Formen verwendet werden. Die Voraussetzung für die Verwendung eines Verbs in der Verlaufsform ist allerdings, dass es eine Handlung ausdrückt, die von einer gewissen „Dauer“ sein muss.

Kurze Handlungen (*to start, to finish, to drop, to see, to hear* usw.) sowie Zustände, Gefühle und sonstige „Nichthandlungen“ (z. B. *to have, to own, to contain, to owe, to like, to feel, to want* usw.) werden fast nie in der *progressive form* ausgedrückt.

Eine nützliche Aufzählung solcher Verben findest du auf S. 28.

Love Story?

A light rain was falling when I reached the station. I was going home after my first term at university, and I was feeling very happy. At the time I was studying in Edinburgh and still living with my parents in London. I was very much looking forward to going home because my girlfriend Hilary would be meeting me at Kings Cross Station. It was December – almost Christmas time. Many of my friends were travelling south on the same train, and there were a lot of well-known – and even more half-known – faces on the platform at Edinburgh's Waverley Station that morning as we waited for the Flying Scotsman. The train would be very crowded.

It was while I was looking for a seat that I saw her. My heart stopped. The girl of my dreams was sitting there reading a paperback novel, and opposite her was one of the few empty seats on the train. We were still standing at the platform. Other young people were putting their bags and suitcases between the seats or on the luggage racks. Nobody seemed to have seen the empty seat – or the girl – except me. "Is this seat taken?" I heard myself ask. I couldn't believe it was actually me speaking. She looked up, smiled and said: "No. I was keeping this seat free for my boyfriend, but he hasn't arrived yet." I sat down opposite her, wondering what to say next. Just then the train began to move. I watched the platform slide backwards as the train gathered speed, and as I was watching I suddenly saw a young man with a heavy suitcase. He was running after the train. Was this her belated boyfriend? Only I could see him. She was facing the other way. But the train was travelling quite fast now, so he couldn't manage to catch it.

Before five minutes had passed Sheila (that was her name) and I were talking as if we had known each other for years. In those days it took five hours to travel from Edinburgh to London, even on a train like the Flying Scotsman, which only stopped at Newcastle. By the time we were passing through York I knew that I had found myself a new girlfriend.

Sheila didn't actually live in London, but she was staying with an uncle and aunt over Christmas. We exchanged addresses and telephone numbers and promised each other that we would meet at some pub for a few drinks at the earliest opportunity. I had forgotten Hilary.

We were ten minutes late at Kings Cross. I helped Sheila off the train with her luggage. She smiled and suddenly put her arms around my neck to kiss me goodbye. I looked up from the kiss and saw that Hilary was walking quickly along the platform towards us.

She was not smiling.

1

Lies die Geschichte "Love Story" genau durch und schreibe die Textstellen heraus, die kontrastierende Formen der Vergangenheit enthalten.
Du kannst so vorgehen:

Simple	Progressive
	A light rain **was falling**
when I **reached** the station.	
I **read** the magazine	while I **was waiting.**

2

Make a list of the past progressive forms in the text and put them into the following categories:

Background description	was ...-ing = *wollte*
...	...

3

Put the two halves of the sentences together.

1. She was talking to me when	a) they met at the pub.
2. Before the robber entered the bank	b) the girls were watching TV.
3. When we went on holiday	c) she was wearing a mask.
4. John talked to Sheila when	d) all our clothes were stolen.
5. First they bought the tickets, then	e) the train arrived.
6. While we were playing tennis	f) the dog stole the sausages.
7. The boys grilled the meat while	g) the phone rang.
8. When I last saw the bank robber	h) they got on the train.
9. They were on the platform when	i) we always locked all the doors.
10. The boys were grilling the meat when	j) she put a mask on.

Du wirst erkannt haben, dass *while* (= während) logischerweise mit der *progressive form* und *when* (= als) mit der *simple form* verwendet wird. Es gibt Ausnahmen, aber du kannst dich normalerweise auf diese Faustregel verlassen.

4

Use the verbs below to complete the following sentences. Each verb should be used **twice**: once in the simple form and once in the progressive form.

say **talk** **wait** **do** **have** **see**

1. "We ______________________ twenty-five minutes for a Number 68 bus yesterday.
2. While we ______________________ , three Number 196 buses came by." –
3. "What __________ you __________ to the conductor when the bus arrived?" –
4. "Nothing. Sue ______________________ to me non-stop.
5. I couldn't hear what anybody else ______________________ ." –
6. "I ________________ Sue in town yesterday. She wasn't at school.
7. Have you any idea what she ______________________ there?" –
8. "She wants to leave school this summer. She ______________________ someone about a job in a bank.
9. She ______________________ to the bank manager for over an hour." –
10. "What __________ she __________ after her interview?" –
11. "She ______________________ a cup of coffee at a café." –
12. "That's right. When I saw her she ______________________ a cup of coffee."

5

Tell the story. Write one sentence for each picture. Use one simple form and one progressive form for each picture and start each sentence with the word above or below the picture, like this:

While I was walking to school one morning, I saw an accident.

1. While I...

2. Just as I...

3. When the police...

4. While...

5. While...

6. Just as...

7. While the driver...

Simple past oder *past progressive*?

Das *simple past* drückt eine oder mehrere relativ kurze Handlungen aus, die in einem abgeschlossenen Zeitraum passierte(n).

Das *past progressive* wird verwendet, um Handlungen in der Vergangenheit auszudrücken, die sozusagen als Hintergründe zu wichtigeren Handlungen „am Ablaufen" sind:

It **was raining** when we **arrived**.	Es **regnete**, als wir **ankamen**. (Regen bildet den Hintergrund)
It **rained** when we **arrived**.	Es **regnete**, als wir **ankamen**. (plötzlich einsetzender Regen)

Achte bei Fragestellungen also immer darauf, was du wissen willst!

Frage nach der „ausgelösten" nächsten Tätigkeit – *simple past*:

What **did** you **do** when the police arrived?	Was **machtest** du, als die Polizei ankam?
I **ran** away.	Ich **lief** weg.

Frage nach der im Augenblick ausgeübten Tätigkeit, als etwas passierte – *past progressive*:

What **were** you **doing** when the police arrived?	Was **machtest** du (gerade), als die Polizei ankam?
I **was sitting** in the living room.	Ich **saß** (gerade) im Wohnzimmer.

Fast immer stehen also beide Zeitformen kontrastiv zueinander in einem Satz und drücken jeweils den Hintergrund *(past progressive)* und die wichtigere Handlung *(simple past)* aus. Stehen zwei Verben im *past progressive* in einem Satz, wird die Gleichzeitigkeit von zwei längeren Handlungen beschrieben:

While I **was watching** TV, my friends **were waiting** for me outside the disco.	Während **ich fern sah**, (= **dabei** war, fernzusehen), **warteten** meine Freunde vor der Disko auf mich.

Wie geht die "Love Story" von Aufgabe 1 weiter? Setze die richtigen Formen – *simple past* oder *past progressive* – der angegebenen Verben in die Sätze ein.

to hope   to talk   to lie (lügen)   to practise   to get

to say   to want   to look   to believe   to have

1. "Hello, Hilary," I ______________________.
2. I ______________________ to kiss her, but she wouldn't let me.
3. "Who was that girl you ______________________ to?" she asked.
4. "Girl? What girl?" I still ______________________ that she hadn't seen us kissing.
5. "The girl on the train. You ______________________ as if you were good friends!"
6. "Oh, you mean Sheila! She's an old friend of mine." – "Old enough to kiss like that?" – I ______________________ to think quickly:
7. "We're both in the university drama club. We're doing 'Brief Encounter' (*„Flüchtige Begegnung", ein berühmtes Bühnenstück)* next term. There's a scene in the play where the hero says goodbye to the heroine at a station. We ______________________ the scene."
8. I could see she __________ n't ______________________ me.
9. She knew that I ______________________.
10. I ______________________ really worried now. "Give me a kiss!" I said. "On one condition," said Hilary. "I want you to promise to send me a ticket for 'Brief Encounter'. I'd love to see the play with you two in it!"

4 *Present perfect* oder *simple past*?

Wann verwende ich *simple past*, wann *present perfect*?

Simple past	**Present perfect**
1. wenn ein Zeitraum in der Vergangenheit erwähnt wird:	nicht erwähnt wird:
We **went** there last week.	We **have been** there.
Where **were** you last night?	Where **have** you **been**? You're wet through!
2. wenn der Zeitpunkt in der Vergangenheit wichtiger ist als die Tatsache selbst: When **did** they **arrive**? – At six o'clock.	
3. wenn eine Handlung nicht in der Vergangenheit, sondern in der Gegenwart endet:	They**'ve** just **arrived**. I**'ve finished** my work.
4. wenn eine in der Vergangenheit begonnene Handlung in die Gegenwart und vermutlich darüber hinaus weitergeführt wird:	We**'ve** always **lived** here.
5. wenn mehrere Handlungen in der Vergangenheit (z.B. in einer Geschichte) aufeinander folgen: I **woke** up, **washed**, **dressed** and **had** breakfast before I **left** for school.	

Das ***present perfect*** wird außerdem benutzt,

1. für Handlungen, die in der Gegenwart zu Ende gehen:
   The rain **has** just **stopped**.
   Signalwörter: *now, (only) just*

2. für abgeschlossene Handlungen, die sich in der Vergangenheit ereigneten, aber keine Zeitangabe enthalten:
   We **have** often **had** a meal in that snack-bar.
   Signalwörter:
   often, several times

3. für Ereignisse, die noch nicht passiert sind *(not ... yet)*, aber noch passieren könnten.

   Signalwörter: *ever?, not ... yet*

Das ***simple past*** wählst du also nicht nach dem Kriterium „abgeschlossene Handlung", sondern nur für Handlungen in abgeschlossenen Zeiträumen der Vergangenheit, auch wenn diese Zeiträume einem Menschenleben oder einem Abschnitt der Geschichte gleichkommen.
Vergleiche:

She never **visited** the USSR.	She **hasn't visited** Russia yet.
(Das Land existiert nicht mehr.)	*(noch nicht passiert)*

Bradford's culture clash

Violent confrontations between police and Asian youths provoked widespread shock last weekend.

Over the past few years Asians in Britain, particularly Muslims, have felt very worried about the way in which the wider culture of drugs, small crime, prostitution and the exploitation of women has invaded the areas where they live.
Drug-taking has increased within the Asian community, and there have been many cases of crimes connected with the drug-taking habit. A sex magazine with photos of Asian girls has been in circulation for over a year, and a gay magazine for Asians has just appeared and is selling well.
All this undermines the traditional values and family life of the Muslim community, and has generated a climate of moral panic.
Because the family is vital to the success of the Asian middle class, the moral threat to the family is also an economic threat.
Many Asians living in city centres have found that the value of their houses goes down when the area becomes known as a centre for drugs and prostitution.
Muslims have started a campaign to protect themselves against these negative features of the outside culture. The campaign began in Birmingham last year. When repeated complaints to the police and local authorities produced no results, Asians set up vigilante groups to clean up the areas. This display of "civic responsibility" has, however, involved Muslims in the criticism by white fellow citizens that they are "anti-liberal". This has led to a conflict of values and ways of life.
This conflict need not lead to violence, but often does. Unemployment is high among Asian young people. Many of them have left school without adequate qualifications, job prospects are poor, and there is still much discrimination in all areas of life.
Young Asians have taken over the moral and religious campaign of the older generation and made it more militant. But they are also more liberal than their parents: they have adopted Western values such as the equality of the sexes, greater freedom of choice where marriage and jobs are concerned, and are thus not only often in conflict with "Western" society but also with the older members of the Asian community. The violent confrontation with police in Bradford last weekend showed that the older generation of Asians is no longer in control of Asian youth in Britain.

(adapted from The Independent, 1995)

1

Read the text from a British daily paper, and list all the forms of the simple past and present perfect under the following headings:

1. Simple past – completed period of time is given or is clear from the context
2. Present perfect – action still going on
3. Present perfect – action (or actions) completed at an undefined time in the past
4. Present perfect – action takes place in the present or very close to the present

2

Make ten sensible sentences. Use the verbs below. Look out for any key words which influence the choice of tense (yesterday, not … yet, etc.). Make at least two questions and two negative sentences for each tense.

play **visit** **eat** **listen to** **drink** **watch**

Examples: Have you ever eaten fish and chips?
I watched a horror film on TV last night.

Have you Did you I We I have We have I/We didn't	ever never often …	…	the radio yesterday evening "hide and seek" as a child/children beer when I/we/you was/were younger a horror film on TV last night football London last year fish and chips Frankfurt yet pop concerts on the radio marmalade when I/we/you were in England

3

Here are some pairs of similar sentences. Each sentence contains one good reason for the choice of tense. Don't forget: choose the simple past for actions in completed periods of time in the past, not just for completed actions. Use the present perfect in all cases where the time in the past is not stated or implied:

1. **(go)** Where's John? – He … to school.
   Where's Jenny? – She … to school five minutes ago.
2. **(live)** I … here all my life.
   Goethe … there for many years.
3. **(do)** … you … your English homework last night?
   … you … your English homework?
4. **(drive)** We … not … to Brighton at the weekend.
   We … not … to Brighton since last year.
5. **(learn)** My sister … to drive a car last year.
   I … not … to drive a car yet.
6. **(write)** Shakespeare … a lot of plays.
   The young author … three plays already.
7. **(buy)** "Look! Our neighbours … a new car!"
   – "Oh! Our neighbours … two new bicycles on Monday.
   They haven't got a car."
8. **(drink)** "… you often … wine?" – "No, not often."
   "… you often … wine when you lived in France?" – "Yes."
9. **(fly)** "… Julie ever … to America?" – "Not yet."
   "When … she … to Australia?" – "In 1994."
10. **(see)** "… you … Patrick this morning?" (at 11.55)
    "… you … Patrick this morning?" (at 12.05)

Achtung:
Eine gemeine Falle hat man dir im Satz 4 gestellt! Die Angabe *since last year* bezieht sich auf einen Zeitabschnitt, der im vorigen Jahr zwar anfängt, jedoch bis in die Gegenwart andauert (und vermutlich bis auf Weiteres andauern wird). Also: *present perfect*. Die Angabe *last year* im darauf folgenden Satz bezieht sich auf das ganze Jahr als abgeschlossene Zeitspanne. Also: *simple past*. Die Frage bei 10. wird auch um fünf vor zwölf (wo Patrick noch auftauchen könnte) anders gestellt als um fünf nach zwölf, wo der Vormittag bereits vorbei ist.

Die falsche Verwendung der Zeitformen im Englischen rührt oft daher, dass du versuchst, eine Zeitform, die in deiner Muttersprache „völlig richtig" eingesetzt wird, auch im Englischen zu benutzen.

Beispiel:

Ich **wohne** in München.	= I **live** in Munich.
Ich **wohne** seit fünf Jahren in München.	= I **have lived** in Munich for five years.

Was ist nun hier los? Im Deutschen wird die „einfache Gegenwart" in beiden Sätzen verwendet. Das stimmt. Aber im Deutschen stellt diese Zeitform nur den Bezug zur Gegenwart (= dauert noch an) her. Die deutsche Perfektform („Ich habe … gelebt…") kann hier nicht – wie im Englischen – für Handlungen verwendet werden, die in der Vergangenheit anfangen und bis in die Gegenwart andauern. Nun eine kurze Übung, die speziell auf dieses Übersetzungsproblem eingeht.

4

Translate the following sentences into English. Don't translate word for word. Think about the correct tense.

1. **Wir haben diesen Film zweimal gesehen.**
2. **Wir haben diesen Film letzte Woche gesehen.**
3. **Er wohnte in Berlin, als ich ihn kannte.**
4. **Meine Tante arbeitet in einem Büro.**
5. **Mein Onkel arbeitet seit 1990 in England.**
6. **Unser Lehrer hat England dreimal besucht.**
7. **Er wohnt hier seit vier Jahren.**
8. **Er hat hier ein Jahr gewohnt, bevor er in die USA ging.**
9. **Sie ist gerade angekommen.**
10. **Sie kommt immer pünktlich an.**

Wenn du diese zehn Sätze alle richtig hast, kann man dir nur gratulieren! Du hast das Problem gepackt! Es bleiben nur ein paar Punkte zu beachten, die mit dem Einsatz des *present perfect* zusammenhängen. Der heikelste Punkt ist wohl die Unterscheidung *for* und *since* (siehe Kapitel 5.2), die du besonders beachten solltest.

5

Someone has scratched out some words on the notice board. Put them back in.

The Tower of London

The oldest part of the Tower of London, the White Tower, ________ built by William the Conqueror after he became King of England in 1066. The 27-metre-high walls are almost 5 metres thick at the bottom and 3.5 metres thick at the top. During its long history the Tower ________ used as a palace, a prison and a garrison. It has been enlarged many times. Many people ________ imprisoned or executed here, including Anne Boleyn, second wife of Henry VIII, who ________ beheaded here in 1536. Her ghost and many others ________ seen in various parts of the Tower.

6

Complete this text by putting the verbs in brackets into the right tense. But be careful! Sometimes the verb should be in the passive.

1. London **(have)** __________ always __________ a traffic problem.
2. In the 1850s it **(be)** __________ already __________ the biggest city in the world and it **(be)** __________ difficult to get quickly from one side of the town to the other.
3. In those days many people **(work)** __________ in the City, London's financial and commercial centre, which is in the east of London, but they **(not live)** __________________________ near their work: they **(prefer)** __________________________ to live in the healthy suburbs to the west of London.

4. The first underground railway in the world **(build)** ____________________ in 1863
5. It **(call)** ____________________ the Metropolitan Railway, and many underground railways all over the world **(take over)** ____________________ the name "Metro" from the first Underground.
6. The railway **(run)** ____________________ from Paddington Station in what **(be)** ____________________ then West London, to Farringdon Street in the City of London.

7

Jenny and Paul want to go camping for the weekend. Jenny is nearly ready now, but she phones Paul to ask if he has done everything. Look at the pictures and make a dialogue.

Example:

last night
yesterday
this afternoon
just

Present perfect oder *simple past* ?

Weit verbreiteter Irrglaube: „Das englische *simple past* wird für abgeschlossene, fertige Handlungen benutzt." Falsch! Das ***simple past*** wird nur für Handlungen **in abgeschlossenen Zeiträumen** benutzt, z. B.

1. wenn ein abgeschlossener Zeitraum erwähnt wird:
   We **saw** her in London **last week**. — Wir haben sie letzte Woche in London gesehen. Wir sahen sie letzte Woche in London.
2. wenn man eine solche Zeitangabe erfragt (Signalwort: *When?*):
   When did you last **see** her? — Wann hast du sie zuletzt gesehen? Wann sahst du sie zuletzt?
3. wenn klar ist, dass ein abgeschlossener Zeitraum im Spiel ist:
   We **went** to the Queen Mum's funeral. — Wir sind auf die Trauerfeier für die Königin Mutter gegangen. (im Jahr 2002)
4. wenn man eine Geschichte erzählt: Alle Geschichten spielen sich in abgeschlossenen Zeiträumen ab.

Wie die Beispiele zeigen, wird das deutsche Perfekt oft in Situationen eingesetzt, wo im Englischen nur das *simple past* verwendet wird. Achtung Fehlerquelle!

Das ***present perfect*** setzt du in fast allen anderen Fällen richtig ein, z. B.

1. wenn die Handlung noch nicht fertig ist (also kein abgeschlossener Zeitraum):
   I**'ve lived** here for five years. — Ich wohne seit fünf Jahren hier. **(Vorsicht!** Präsens im Deutschen!)
2. wenn die Handlung in der Gegenwart abgeschlossen wird (daher der Name *present perfect):*
   She **has** just **finished** reading it. — Sie hat es gerade zu Ende gelesen.
3. wenn gefragt wird, *ob* etwas passiert ist, nicht *wann* es möglicherweise passierte:
   Has he **read** this book? — Hat er dieses Buch gelesen?
4. wenn gesagt wird, *dass* etwas passiert ist, und uninteressant ist, *wann* es passierte:
   They **have** often **visited** Britain. — Sie haben Großbritannien oft besucht. ODER: Sie **waren** oft in Großbritannien.

Nur bei Punkt 1 handelt es sich um eine nicht abgeschlossene Handlung!

Vervollständige diesen Dialog mit den in Klammern stehenden Wörtern. Die Zeitbestimmungen geben dir Aufschluss über die zu verwendende Zeitform, müssen aber in einigen Fällen an der richtigen Stelle in den Satz eingebaut werden.

1. (to be, ever) "__________ you __________ to Scotland?"
2. (to be, 2001) "Yes, I __________________ there in __________. And you?"
3. (to be, never) "No, I ______________________________ there.
4. (to book, just) But I ______________________________ an English course in Edinburgh.
5. (to see) I ______________________ an advertisement for English courses in the newspaper a few days ago. 'English in Scotland' is the name of the company."
6. (to see, often) "Oh! I ______________________________ that advertisement.
7. (to go, already) A friend of mine __________________________ on several 'English in Scotland' courses.
8. (to tell) She ______________________ me all about them when I last saw her.
9. (to seem) She ________n't ______________________ very happy about the accommodation (Unterbringung).
10. (to enjoy) but she ______________________ the courses very much."

5 Das *present perfect:* *simple* oder *progressive form* ?

5.1 *Simple present perfect* und *present perfect progressive* im Vergleich

Das *present perfect progressive* wird nur bei Verben eingesetzt, die einen zeitlichen Verlauf darstellen (z. B.: *live, work, wait, play, watch TV* usw.):

We **have been living** here since 1980.

Nicht aber bei Verben, die nur kurze Handlungen beschreiben (*finish, stop, decide, want* usw.) und deshalb fast immer in der *simple form* verwendet werden. Vergleiche:

There you are! I**'ve finished** my homework at last.
I**'ve been working** at it all afternoon!

Bei Verben, die sowohl in der Verlaufs- als auch in der einfachen Form benutzt werden können, betont die Verlaufsform die Dauer einer Handlung, während die einfache Form die Tatsache selbst oder das Ergebnis betont:

She **has been working** in the garden all day.
She **has worked** very hard. Just look at the garden!

Signalwörter:
Da Verben in der *progressive form* einen Handlungsverlauf beschreiben, ist in solchen Sätzen oft die Dauer *(all day, all my life, for ten years)* bzw. der Ausgangspunkt (*since 1992* usw.) angegeben.

1

Give the reasons why. You will need the present perfect progressive form in all your sentences.

Example: "I'm sorry my hands are dirty but…" **(repair/car)**
"I'm sorry my hands are dirty but I've been repairing my car."

1. "You look hot!" – "Yes, that's because …" **(play/football)**
2. "She doesn't speak much English even though …" **(live in London/three years already)**
3. "How long …?" **(you/wait/here)** – "About an hour."
4. "My bottle of whisky is almost empty. I think …!" **(someone/drink/it)**
5. "Let's stop. We …" **(practise/English grammar/3 o'clock)**
6. "What … ?" **(she/do/all afternoon)** – "Playing tennis."
7. "I'm sorry, but I can't go to the cinema tonight." – "Oh! I'm so disappointed! …!" **(look forward to it/all week)**
8. "…?" **(the baby/behave/well)** – "Oh, yes. So far, at least."

2

Put the most likely form of the verb in brackets (present perfect simple or progressive) into the following sentences:

1. **(learn)** "… you … ten new words today?"
2. **(learn)** "How long … you … English?" – "Four years."
3. **(see)** "I …n't … John since last week."
4. **(see)** "John … Stephanie a lot recently. They're very good friends."
5. **(have)** "They … lunch for over an hour already."
6. **(have)** "They … never … real English food."
7. **(work)** "She hasn't had much free time recently because she … on her school geography project."
8. **(work)** "What a wonderful exam result! You … very hard!"
9. **(do)** "What … you … all afternoon?" (listen) – "I … to my CDs."
10. **(do)** "The cassette recorder I lent you doesn't work! What … you … to it?"
11. **(watch)** "You look tired. … you … too much TV again?"
12. **(watch)** "They … the birds in the garden all morning."
13. **(be)** "… you ever … to Gobowen?" – "Where on earth is Gobowen?"

5.2 Der Gebrauch von *for, since* und *ago*

For und *since* (beide = „seit", beide besonders häufige Signalwörter für das *present perfect progressive*), sind sowohl voneinander als auch von der deutschen Präposition „vor … Jahren/Tagen" zu unterscheiden, das im Englischen mit … *years/days ago* übersetzt wird.

seit = ***since*** + Zeit**punkt**:	I've known her **since** 1988/last week.
seit = ***for*** + Zeit**spanne**:	I've known her **for** three weeks/a few days.
vor= Zeit**punkt** + ***ago***:	She lived here three years **ago**.

Da *ago* immer einen Zeitpunkt in der Vergangenheit markiert, steht das Verb fast immer im *simple past*:
I met her three days ago.

Eine scheinbare Ausnahme bildet die Kombination von ***since*** *(two years)* ***ago***, die eine Zeit**spanne** bezeichnet:

I've known her **for** three weeks.	(Zeitspanne)
I've known her **since** last month.	(Zeitpunkt)
I've known her **since three weeks ago**.	(Zeitspanne = seit vor drei Wochen)

Da *since* den Anfangszeitpunkt einer Handlung markiert, die bis in die Gegenwart hineinreicht, steht das Verb davor immer im *present perfect*.

Since wird mit dem *simple past* nur in Nebensätzen benutzt, wo das Verb den Anfangszeitpunkt der Handlung beschreibt. Ein Verb im Nebensatz nach *since* steht also immer im *simple past*.

Vergleiche:
She came to London in February.
I**'ve known** her **since February**.
I**'ve known** her **since** she **came** to London. (= since February)

3

Make ten sentences from the switchboard using "for, since, ago" and "since … ago". Use each construction at least twice:

1. John 2. We 3. She 4. They 5. Peter and Sophia	have has	been learning lived been working	here English	… last June. … three years … … six weeks. … three months … … they left Berlin. …
		came lived		

4

Complete the following sentences: "for, since, from, ago"

1. ____________ years Christine Meadows wanted to work on a railway.
2. Her wish came true six months ____________.
3. Christine has now been working at Gobowen station ____________ last September, ____________ she became a sixth-former, in fact.
4. Railways are in the family. Christine's uncle worked as an engine-driver ____________ 1965 until he retired in 1995.
5. ____________ his retirement, Joe Meadows has been working as part-time station-master on a private tourist railway in North Wales.
6. ____________ six hours a day during the summer season he sells tickets at the station.
7. Joe works ____________ 10 a.m. to 5 p.m. with an hour for lunch.
8. The railway, which was built over 150 years ____________, once transported slate *(= Schiefer)* from the mountains to the sea.
9. But ____________ the 1950s it has been a big tourist attraction, and now it only transports passengers.
10. No slate has been transported on it ____________ sixty years ago.

5

Look at the pictures and write a local TV news report about the young men who want to take over the bus service to a small Scottish village. Use a form of the present perfect in all the sentences.

1 Last week the Highland Bus Company decided to close down the bus service from Aviemore to the remote Highland village of Strathdon, even though this service … fifty years.

2 The people of Strathdon are very angry. They say …
One woman says …

3 Our reporter Samantha Bevis is in Strathdon tonight. She is talking to some of the villagers. "…?" – "…"

4 "What are you going to do?" – "Well, we …

5 We'll run the service ourselves. I'm a bus-driver. I …" – "Yes. I think I'm a good driver because …

6 and …"

7 "The villagers of Strathdon …

8 A representative of the bus company … I'll try and have a few words with him after the meeting."

9 "Has the meeting been a success?" – "Well, not really. We … but no real progress …

10 If the young men of the village want to run the bus service we think they should have a try. The bus company …"

6

Put yourself in the following situations. How would you react?

Situation	Reaction
Example: You see a friend who has shaved his (or her) head. He (or she) is completely bald! You say: *"What have you done to your hair?"*	do?
1. You can't find your school-bag. You think your mother might know where it is.	see?
2. You bought yourself a bar of chocolate yesterday. Today there is only half a bar left. You ask your brothers, sisters or friends.	eat?
3. Even worse! All the chocolate is gone – only the wrapper is left!	who / eat?
4. You haven't seen Douglas Smith for some time. Perhaps he doesn't live in your town any more. You ask a schoolfriend.	see / recently?
5. You are late for a date with your boyfriend/girlfriend. You run all the way to the disco, but he/she is already there.	wait / long?
6. There was an article in the newspaper about the oldest man (97) in your town, but you didn't read it. You ask a friend about him.	how long / live here?
7. You are having a party, but your best friend arrives an hour late!	where on earth / be?
8. Someone says "I'm very sorry" to you, but you don't know why.	what / do?
9. Someone arrives at school with very dirty hands.	what on earth / do?
10. You look very tired after this exercise. A friend asks you:	how long / practise / English?

Present perfect: simple oder *progressive form*?

Die *simple form* des *present perfect* betont eine Tatsache, die *progressive form* betont dagegen den ununterbrochenen Verlauf einer Handlung:

Present perfect simple	Present perfect progressive
I**'ve worked** at Smiths for 20 years. *Ich arbeite bei Smiths seit 20 Jahren. (Tatsache)*	I**'ve been working** hard all day. *Ich arbeite den ganzen Tag hart. (Beschreibung)*
We**'ve asked** him to come tomorrow.	We**'ve been asking** him to come since February!
Wir haben ihn gebeten, morgen zu kommen.	*Wir bitten ihn schon seit Februar zu kommen!* (Im Deutschen: Präsens!)

Ein besonderes Problem beim *present perfect simple* oder *progressive* ist die Übersetzung des deutschen Wortes „seit". Im Englischen wird *for* bei Zeit**spannen** (so viele Jahre, Monate, Wochen, Tagen), *since* bei Zeit**angaben** (Jahreszahl, Monatsname, Wochentag, Uhrzeit) benutzt. Außerdem kann *since* einen Nebensatz anführen, der die Zeitangabe beschreibt:

I**'ve worked / been working** at Smiths **for** over 20 years. **Since** 1984, in fact.
Ich arbeite *bei Smiths seit über 20 Jahren. Eigentlich seit 1984*

He**'s known** her **for** years. **Since** 1998, I think. **Since** she moved here, in fact.
Er ***kennt*** *sie seit Jahren. Seit 1998, glaube ich. Eigentlich seitdem sie hierher gezogen ist.*

Im Deutschen wird „seit" (da deutlich gesagt werden muss, dass die Handlung in der Gegenwart noch ausgeübt wird) mit dem Präsens benutzt. Im Englischen zeigt das *present perfect* an, dass eine Handlung, die in der Vergangenheit begann, noch in der Gegenwart fortgesetzt wird.

Das englische Präsens wird **nie** mit *for/since* verwendet, das deutsche Präsens in solchen Fällen aber **immer** mit „seit"!

Eine weitere Fehlerquelle:
Verwechsle nie das englische *for* mit dem deutschen „vor"!

She came to Germany three weeks **ago**.
Sie kam **vor** drei Wochen nach Deutschland.

She came to Germany **for** three weeks.
Sie kam **für** drei Wochen nach Deutschland.

Warum hat Leonard schon wieder eine 5 geschrieben?
Findest du seine Fehler? Nur zwei Sätze in dieser Klassenarbeit waren richtig. Also überlege gut, bevor du einen Satz korrigierst!

1. I didn't finish my homework yet.

   ____

2. She has phoned her boyfriend for half an hour.

   ____

3. We live here since 2001

   ____

4. My friend Peter has been living in London since three years ago.

   ____

5. I have done my homework all afternoon. I need a break.

   ____

6. Our English teacher has started at our school three years ago.

   ____

7. He has only been knowing her for three days.

   ____

8. I met her for two years.

   ____

9. How long have the children been watching that programme on TV?

   ____

10. We know them for three months.

   ____

6 Das *past perfect*

6.1 *Simple past* oder *past perfect*?

Simple past und *past perfect* im Satzgefüge

Das *past perfect* sorgt für Klarheit in der Handlungsreihenfolge in der Vergangenheit:

He **rang** the doorbell because he **had forgotten** his key.
Jenny **got** up, **walked** to the window and **looked** out. It **had snowed** in the night.

Vergleiche die Reihenfolge:

1 2
When we **arrived**, John **made** lunch.
2 1
When we **arrived**, John **had made** lunch.

Im ersten Satz wird die zeitliche Reihenfolge und die unmittelbare Nähe der Handlungen durch die Verwendung derselben Zeitform festgehalten.
Im zweiten Satz hatte John das Mittagessen bereits gemacht, bevor wir ankamen. Die Reihenfolge im Satz ist umgekehrt, aber die Verwendung des *past perfect* schließt Missverständnisse aus.

Die beiden Satzteile im ersten Beispiel können aber auch vertauscht werden, ohne dass ein Missverständnis entsteht:

John **made** lunch when we **arrived**.

Im Satz „John **made** lunch **after** we **had arrived**."
nimmt man an, dass eine längere Pause und eventuell auch andere, nicht erwähnte Aktivitäten dazwischenkamen.

Das *past perfect* wird auch nach when im Sinne von *after* benutzt:
Vergleiche:

When he **had told** me his story, he **asked** me to lend him some money.
(eine Handlung vor der nächsten beendet: when = *nachdem)*
When he **told** me his story, I **was** shocked.
(ich war evtl. auch während des Erzählens bereits schockiert: when = *als, während)*
When I **saw** Derek last week, he **had shaved** his beard off.
(er hatte seinen Bart bereits abrasiert: when = *als)*

Auch *until* (= erst als, bis) wird mit dem *past perfect* benutzt:

Mum didn't let me watch TV **until** I **had finished** my homework.

Signalwörter für *past perfect*: *after, when (= after), until* (= erst als)

1

Use "after" to join the two halves of the sentences like this:

Shirley did her homework. Then she took her dog for a walk.
After Shirley had done her homework, she took her dog for a walk.

Mr Wilson marked our test. But he took his dog for a walk first.
Mr Wilson marked our test after he had taken his dog for a walk.

1. Patricia passed her driving test. She bought a car.
2. She drove home, locked the car and went into the house.
3. First Patricia made a cup of coffee. Then she phoned her friend Anna.
4. She put down the phone. But first she said goodbye to Anna.
5. She looked out of the window because she heard a loud noise.
6. Two young men were trying to steal her car radio. They broke a window to get into the car.
7. Patricia realized what was happening. She rang the police.
8. Her neighbour came out of his house. He heard the noise.
9. The man shouted something. The boys looked up and saw him.
10. They ran away. A police car arrived outside Patricia's house.

2

Now join the two sentences with "when", but remember: sometimes you will need the past perfect tense.

1. He told me his name. I knew who he was.
2. We finished lunch. We went for a walk.
3. She wiped her feet on the doormat. She shut the front door.
4. He took the dog for a walk. It was very cold outside.
5. Our teacher gave us the dictation. He collected our exercise books.
6. My mum learnt Russian. She went to school in East Germany.
7. The sun set. The stars came out.
8. I lit a match. The lights went out.
9. He tried to speak French. Everybody laughed.
10. All my friends were on holiday. I felt very lonely.

3

Jane and Alan went on a trip round the USA last July. Here is her diary.

Mon 1	*Flight London – New York: booked into hotel in Manhattan*
Tues 2	*Sightseeing trip round Manhattan: –> Statue of Liberty*
Wed 3	*NYC ...*
Thurs 4	*Celebrated Independence Day in New York City!*
Fri 5	*–> by car to Washington*
Sat 6	*Sights of Washington –> Disneyworld (Orlando, Florida)*
Sun 7	}
Mon 8	} *Spent 2 days in Florida –> Flew to Arizona*
Tue 9	*Visited Grand Canyon & Yosemite National Park*
Wed 10	}
Thurs 11	} *Drove over the Rockies to San Francisco*
Fri 12	*Stayed with friends there*
Sat 13	*Saw Golden Gate Bridge and other sights –> Seattle (plane)*
Sun 14	}
Mon 15	} *Two days in Seattle with friends of Alan's –> London via Chicago*
Tue 16	
Wed 17	
Thurs 18	*Recovered from the jet lag (at last!) – felt much better!*

After the trip, Jane told her friends about what they had done. What did she say?
Start like this: *After we had flown from London to New York, we ...*

In some sentences you can use "when" instead of "after", but not in all of them.

Signalwort *before + past perfect*

before + past perfect drückt eine erste Handlung aus, die nicht vor Einsetzen der nächsten Handlung beendet werden konnte.

Vergleiche:

I **read** several books about the USA before I **went** there.
She **gave** me the book back before she **had finished** it.
He **finished** speaking when/just as three armed men **rushed** into the room. Before he **had finished** speaking, three armed men rushed into the room.

Die Verwendung von *before* und *after* entsprechen dem deutschen Gebrauch von „bevor" und „nachdem".

4

Join the two sentences with "before" – but be careful! You only need the past perfect with "before" if the first action could not be completed before the second action started. Leave out any words in brackets.

1. He couldn't finish his lunch. His guests arrived.
2. She bought a newspaper. The train left.
3. We put warm clothes on. We went out into the snow.
4. The boy jumped off. The bus didn't stop.
5. The TV programme started. We finished our homework.
6. We reached home. Then it began to rain.
7. They didn't reach the bus station (in time). The bus left.
8. She left school. She didn't finish her course.
9. They left New York. They didn't have time to see the Statue of Liberty.
10. We didn't start to eat. The others arrived.

6.2 Der Gebrauch des *past perfect progressive*

Wann verwende ich das *past perfect progressive*?

1. Für Handlungen in Zeiträumen, die bis in die Gegenwart hineinreichen und die meist mit *for* oder *since* angegeben werden, wird in der Gegenwart das *present perfect progressive*, in der Vergangenheit das *past perfect progressive* verwendet.
   Vergleiche:
   I **had** just **switched** the TV on when mum **came** in.
   I **had** only **been watching** for five minutes when mum **switched** it off.
   (*direkte Rede:* "Mum! **I've** only **been watching** for five minutes!")
   Sue **had been working** there since 1992 when she **met** Colin.
   ("I**'ve been working** here since 1992," Sue said to Colin when they met.)

   Vergleiche auch:
   I **was watching** TV when mum **came** in and **switched** it off.
   Sue **was working** there when she **met** Colin.

   Hier wird keine Zeitspanne angegeben.

   Die Verlaufsform wird vor allen Dingen bei Verben benutzt, die Handlungen von längerer Dauer ausdrücken: *to live, to work, to wait, to watch, to play, to listen* usw.

2. Für wiederholte Handlungen in einem ähnlichen Zeitrahmen.
   Vergleiche:
   He **had been trying** to phone his girlfriend for half an hour before he got through. He said to her: "**I've been trying** to phone you for half an hour!"

Im Gegensatz zur *simple form* des *past perfect*, die auf ein fertiges Ergebnis hindeutet, drückt die *progressive form* nicht unbedingt aus, dass die Tätigkeit abgeschlossen ist, sondern zeigt eher an, wie man die Zeit zugebracht hat:

She **had typed** all the letters, so she could go home.
She **had been typing** all afternoon, so she was very tired.

5

Johnny Brown, the famous pop singer, is giving one of his rare interviews about his career.The reporter's tape recorder was not working, so he had to write down the information in note form. Can you write the full story for him? Use the progressive form with "after" or "when" as often as possible. (It isn't always needed.)

Start like this:

Johnny Brown, the famous pop singer, was born in 1970. After he ...

Born 1970.
Left school 1985 – started work as an assistant in a music shop
Learning to play guitar 3 years – joined the Steve Miller Band
Left after playing only two months
Came to live in New York: 1987 – founded The Konks 3 years later
Group played together for 2 years – broke up
Solved his drug problem – founded a new group The Daws
First concert successful – could only leave stage after six encores *(= Zugaben)*
Made first CD 1994 – fans waited 2 years!
Group worked together 3 years, then broke up in 1996
Gave 20 concerts and made three CDs

"Didn't you tell us that nobody had ever climbed this mountain before?"

Der Gebrauch des *past perfect*

Wenn eine Trennung in der zeitlichen Reihenfolge von zwei Handlungen in der Vergangenheit deutlich hervorgehoben werden soll, wird für die frühere Handlung das englische *past perfect* verwendet. Vergleiche:

When I **arrived**, Susan **left**.	Als ich ankam, ging Susan weg.
When I **arrived**, Susan **had left**.	Als ich ankam, war Susan schon weggegangen.

Im ersten Beispiel hängen die beiden Handlungen unmittelbar zusammen – fast in einem „Ursache-und-Wirkung"-Verhältnis. Es sieht aus, als ob Susan wegging, gerade *weil* ich kam. Vielleicht mag sie mich nicht! Im zweiten Satz haben beide Handlungen gar nichts miteinander zu tun. Auch zeitlich folgen sie nicht unmittelbar aufeinander, und die Reihenfolge wird durch die Verwendung von zwei unterschiedlichen Zeitformen deutlich markiert. Dabei ist es egal, in welcher Reihenfolge die beiden Handlungen im Satz erscheinen.

Signalwörter für das *past perfect*: *after, when (= after), before, until* (= bis, erst als):

After our guests had gone, we washed up.	Nachdem unsere Gäste gegangen waren, machten wir den Abwasch.
I waited **until** John had finished talking.	Ich wartete, bis John aufgehört hatte zu reden.
When he had finished talking, I started.	Als er aufgehört hatte zu reden, fing ich an.
I was interrupted **before** I had finished.	Ich wurde unterbrochen, bevor ich zu Ende gesprochen hatte.

Die *progressive form* des *past perfect* wird verwendet,

- um den Verlauf einer Handlung auszudrücken. Vergleiche:

Simple form:	We **had** always **walked** to the village before the new bus service started up.
Progressive form:	We **had been walking** for ten minutes when the sun came out.

- um zu betonen, dass sich eine Handlung in einem bestimmten Zeitrahmen mehrfach wiederholt hat:
  She **had been trying** to phone the doctor for half an hour before she got through.

Zu weiteren Verwendungen des *past perfect* siehe „Bedingungssätze Typ III" und „Indirekte Rede".

Past perfect, simple past oder *past progressive*? Alle drei Zeitformen hängen mehr oder weniger zusammen. *Past perfect* wird mit *simple past* kombiniert, das *past progressive* ebenfalls. Jetzt wird's Zeit zu prüfen, ob du alle drei Zeitformen – und dazu das *past perfect progressive* – richtig einsetzen kannst. Die angegebenen Verbformen passen in die Sätze – bloß in welche? Beachte immer den Zusammenhang des ganzen Satzes, bevor du deine Wahl triffst. Es sind genauso viele Verbformen, wie du brauchst.

saw went was waiting / had been waiting had taken

had had / had been having read / was reading felt / was feeling

said talked / had been talking walked / was walking

had left / left / had left remembered arrived

1. He … at the station for two hours when the train finally arrived.
2. While he …, he … a magazine.
3. He … an interesting article when the train … .
4. Ten minutes after the train … the station, he … hungry.
5. Because he … hungry, he … his seat and went to the restaurant car *(Speisewagen)*.
6. After he … a snack, he … back to his seat.
7. As he … back to his seat, he … a friend of his.
8. He … hello and … to his friend for while.
9. When he … to his friend for a few minutes,
10. he … that he … his magazine in the restaurant car while he … his snack.

    So he … back to look for it, but it was gone. Someone … it with him.

7 Bedingungssätze

7.1 Bedingungssätze Typ I

Bedingungssätze Typ I

Bei einfachen Bedingungen ist die Bedingung leicht zu erfüllen.
Wenn du etwas tust, tritt etwas anderes unweigerlich ein.

Zeitenfolge:

if-Satz present simple	Hauptsatz *will*-future
If you **help** me with my English,	I'**ll help** you with your Maths.
	Will they come to the meeting
if we **invite** them? –	
	They **won't come**
unless you **invite** them politely!	

Die Reihenfolge der beiden Satzhälften ist unwichtig.
If … not wird besonders dann durch *unless* ersetzt, wenn das Verb im Hauptsatz verneint ist. So werden Verwirrungen durch die Verneinung des Verbs in beiden Satzhälften vermieden.

Die Verlaufsform der Gegenwart kann auch verwendet werden, um zwischen Dauerhandlung *(progressive)* und „Einmalhandlung" zu unterscheiden:

If you'**re** really **looking** for a job, you'**ll find** one.

Im *if*-Satz, Typ I, ist das Verb auch im *present perfect* möglich.

If you **have finished** talking, we **will go** on to the next question.

Achtung:
Verwechsle nicht *if* mit *when*! Im Deutschen wird beides mit „wenn" übersetzt

1

Look at the pictures and use them to complete the sentences below.
Sometimes you have to provide the if-clause, sometimes the main clause.

1. If I ever go to America, ______________________________.
2. We'll come to your party ______________________________.
3. Unless it rains, ______________________ barbecue outside.
4. Our friends won't come unless ______________________________.
5. Boy to girl: "Will you lend me £10 ______________________?"
6. If you aren't learning English, __________ not enjoy ______________.
7. ______________ help me do the washing-up if I ______________ ______________________?
8. I'll go to Spain in summer ______________________________.
9. Unless you __________ the police, the robbers ______________.
10. Unless we ______________, the bull ______________!

Bedingungssätze Typ I mit modalen Hilfsverben im Hauptsatz

Beim einfachen Bedingungssatz Typ I drückt die Zukunftsform im Hauptsatz aus, dass bei Erfüllung der Bedingung das Ergebnis immer eintritt. Mit dem Einsatz anderer modaler Hilfsverben im Hauptsatz (statt *will* z. B. *can, may, might* usw.) können statt der 100%igen Sicherheit des Ergebnisses andere „Modalitäten" (Können, Möglichkeit usw.) ausgedrückt werden.

Vergleiche den einfachen Bedingungssatz Typ I

If we go to New York, we'll visit Manhattan.	(100% certain)

mit:

If we visit Manhattan, we **can** go to the top of the Empire State Building.	(ability)
If we go to the Empire State Building, we **could** have lunch there.	(less likely)
If we have enough time, we **may** visit Harlem.	(possibility)
But if we visit Harlem, we **might** be mugged.	(less likely)
If you are alone in New York, you **must** be careful.	(necessity)
But if you wear your oldest clothes, you **needn't** worry about being mugged.	(no necessity)
You **should** be/**ought to** be safe enough unless you wander down back alleys.	(probability)
If you don't know a person, you **shouldn't** trust him or her.	(advice)
If you remember, **could** you buy me a few postcards of New York?	(request)

2

Read the dialogue and put in modal auxiliaries to suit the context.

1. "What are your plans for the weekend, Sharon?" – "Well, if the weather is good, Dad says we ____________________ go for a drive in the country on Saturday."
2. "That's one possibility. What about a trip to the seaside?" – "I suppose we ____________________ go to Eastbourne if we start early enough. It's a long way, though. What about your plans, Robin?" –
3. "I haven't got any. Do you think you ____________________ take me with you if you go to Eastbourne? I haven't been to the seaside for ages." –
4. "I'll ask Mum and Dad. If there's room in the car, that ________________ be all right." –
5. "Will we have time to go to the top of those high cliffs?" – "You mean Beachy Head? I'm not sure. We ____________________ have time if we don't spend too long on the beach.
6. But if we go right to the top, you ____________________ be very careful! It's very dangerous." –
7. "Will we be back before it gets dark?" – "I expect so. We ______________ get stuck in a traffic jam if we're very unlucky, but that's not very likely. Should I phone you on Friday evening?" –
8. "No, that won't be necessary. If your parents say I can come, you ____________________ phone me. When should I be at your house?" –
9. "Come round after breakfast. If you arrive at about ten, we ____________ leave straight away.
10. We ____________________ leave much later than ten if we want to get back before dark."

7.2 Bedingungssätze Typ II

Bei Sätzen dieses Typs ist die Bedingung oft unerfüllbar: Wenn du etwas tätest, träte eventuell etwas anderes ein. Viele Aussagen des Typs II verbleiben im Bereich des Wunschdenkens.

Zeitenfolge:

if-Satz *simple past* (eigentlich Konjunktiv)	Hauptsatz *would* + Infinitiv (conditional)
If I **had** a bit more time,	I **would read** an English paper.
	We'**d spend** our holidays in Britain
... if it **didn't rain** so much!	
If they **knew** the right answer,	**would** they **tell** us?
If the money **was found**	we **would be given** a reward.

Die Reihenfolge der beiden Satzhälften ist unwichtig. Oft wird guter Rat mit der einzigen noch vorhandenen, englischen Konjunktivform so ausgedrückt:

If I **were** you,	I **wouldn't wait** for the bus. It's quicker to walk.

Die *progressive form* und andere Hilfsverben in beiden Satzhälften (vgl. Kap. 7.1) sind auch möglich:

If I **were** in the office now,	I **would be working** hard.
If I **were learning** Spanish,	I **might go** to Spain.
If my car **were working,**	I **could drive** you home.
If only I **could speak** more French,	I **wouldn't worry** about moving to Paris.

3

Put the halves of the sentences together, but be careful not to mix Type I and Type II sentences.

1.	If the ferry sinks,	a)	you would be punished.
2.	Unless you behave,	b)	we'd all be killed.
3.	If you stole a car,	c)	we wouldn't be sorry.
4.	If our teacher is ill,	d)	I won't let you go to the party.
5.	If the plane crashed,	e)	we'll have to swim.
6.	If the school burned down,	f)	we won't have a test tomorrow.
7.	Will you phone me	g)	if you knew the number?
8.	Would you help them	h)	if I were you!
9.	She'll lend you her book	i)	if you have time?
10.	I'd be more careful	j)	if you ask nicely.

4

Complete the sentences with the right form of the verb in brackets. Watch out for the two passive forms!

Black – and poor – in Britain

1. **(live)** If you are black, you … probably … in one of the inner suburbs of the larger towns. 2. **(know)** If white people … how difficult it was to find jobs, they would realize why young black people sometimes turn to crime. 3. **(do)** There will be no reduction in street crime in Britain unless more … to help the underprivileged. 4. **(be)** … life in the inner cities … better if the slums were pulled down and new flats built? 5. **(find)** Probably not. If we look at the housing projects of the 1950s and 60s we … that the new flats soon became modern slums. 6. **(give)** If blacks … better chances, would they also be better citizens? 7. **(feel)** The answer to that question is clear. Unless they are given equal opportunities, young blacks … that they are being discriminated against. 8. **(think)** If they … they are being discriminated against, they will not trust the police. 9. **(not trust)** They won't consider themselves to be responsible citizens if they … by the police. 10. **(trust)** After all, … you … the police if you were treated like a second-class citizen? I wouldn't!

7.3 Bedingungssätze Typ III

Wenn du etwas getan hättest, wäre etwas anderes eingetreten (oder auch nicht). Da die Bedingung sowieso unerfüllbar ist, verbleiben alle Aussagen des Typs III im Bereich des Wunschdenkens bzw. der verpassten Gelegenheiten.

Zeitenfolge:

if-Satz past perfect (eigentlich Konjunktiv)	Hauptsatz *would have + past participle (= conditional perfect)*
If I **had known** you were coming,	I'**d have baked** a cake.
... if I'**d had** enough of my own.	I **wouldn't have asked** you for money
... if you **had been** in my shoes?	What **would** you **have done**

Die *progressive form* ist auch möglich:

If you **had been paying** attention,	you **would have noticed** the mistake.

Die Reihenfolge der beiden Satzhälften ist unwichtig.

Achtung: „hätte" und „wäre" sind nicht gleich „hätte" bzw. „wäre"

Vergleiche:
Wenn er mir das gleich **gesagt hätte, hätte** ich ihm **verziehen.**
*If he **had told** me that right away, I **would have forgiven** him.*

„Hätte" bleibt *had* im *if*-Teil, weil es sich um eine echte Konjunktivform handelt. Im Hauptsatz aber stellt „hätte" eine Verschmelzung von „würde ... haben" dar. Im Englischen wird die unverkürzte Konstruktion *would have* benutzt.

Dasselbe gilt für „wäre", denn die zusammengesetzten Perfektformen werden im Englischen alle mit *have* gebildet:

Wenn wir früher **gekommen wären, wären** wir auch früher **gegangen.**
*If we **had arrived** earlier, we **would have left** earlier, too.*

5

Read the following article about street crime in Britain and pick out the if-sentences. Put them into separate lists for Types I, II and III. You may shorten the longer sentences. Are there any sentences which do not fit into any of the groups? Put them into a fourth list. We will have a look at them later.

Mugging: criminal or political offence?

If you stand around a London Underground station for long enough, you will probably witness at least one case of mugging. But how would you define mugging if someone asked you to give a definition? The Oxford English Dictionary gives "to mug – to rob with violence, especially in a public place".
So who are the muggers and who are their victims? Sir Paul Condon, London's Police Commissioner, recently stated: "It is a fact that very many of the perpetrators of mugging are very young black people." If he were only talking about Central London, he would probably be right. 70 or 80% of victims mugged in this area would, if asked, describe their attackers as "black". But though not all the victims were "white", it is also a fact that a black is less likely to report a case of mugging if he is mugged by another black, because black citizens distrust the mainly white police.
So, nationally, are most muggers young blacks? No. In Newcastle and Glasgow, cities with few blacks, mugging statistics are not divided up by race, but if they had been, you would probably still find that mugging is very much a white offence.
Is mugging a racially related offence? Again, no. If you study the few statistics available, you will find that most muggings are white on white or black on black. Is mugging a serious offence? Numerically, no. Last year's 33,000 street crimes (a term which includes more than just muggings) only make up 4% of a total of 837,000 crimes. Five times as many car crimes and burglaries were reported as muggings. Even from the financial point of view, a mugging would tend not to be reported unless a lot of money were involved.
So what is all the fuss about? Sir Paul's statement, quoted above, was contained in a letter sent to 40 mainly black community leaders and MPs early in July. If he had thought more carefully about the wording of this letter, which seems to suggest that every young male black is a potential mugger, he would not have caused such a furore. Anyway, how do you define "black"? And do you include Asians? Should you try to stop a mugging if you see one happening? These and many other questions will still have to be answered if a solution to street crime is to be found.

6

Look at the pictures and tell the story. This is a chain exercise (the second half of one sentence gives you the first half of the next). Start like this:

1. John had a motor scooter with worn tyres. If he had listened to his friend Raymond, he would have bought new tyres before going on holiday.
2. If he had bought new tyres, ...
3. If he hadn't had ...

7.4 Mischformen

Manchmal haben Ereignisse in der Vergangenheit Auswirkungen in der Gegenwart. Das führt zu folgenden Mischformen:

Typ II + I

If you **enjoyed** Dragon Quest, (= when you first played it)	you **will love** our new game. (= now)
… unless you **were** at Brighton . (= last year)	You **will** not **remember** me (= now)
If they **have** never **met**, (= so far)	they **won't know** each other. (= now)

Typ III + II

	Would she **be** a famous film star today (= result in the present)
… if she **hadn't met** Alfred Hitchcock in 1976? (= meeting in the past)	

In beiden Satzteilen kann auch die Verlaufsform verwendet werden:

If only I **had listened** to you, (= advice given in the past)	I **would be living** in luxury now! (= result in the present)
	She **would know** the answer
… if she **had been paying** attention.	

Verwechsle nicht *if* mit *when*! Im Deutschen wird beides mit „wenn" übersetzt:

I'll phone you when I return.	Ich rufe dich an, wenn ich zurückkomme.
I'll phone you if I return.	

Merke:
Im Englischen gibt der Nebensatz mit *when* im oben genannten Beispiel den **Zeitpunkt** des Anrufes an, während der Nebensatz mit *if* die **Bedingung** nennt, unter der überhaupt ein Anruf erfolgt.

7

Put the two sentences together as in the examples. Use the progressive forms where necessary:

Examples: Margaret **would not like** German food if she **had not tried** it last year.
If she had failed her exams, she would be repeating a year.

1. I didn't win a prize. I am very unhappy.
2. John is living in London now. He found a job there last year.
3. My friend started learning French a couple of years ago. He spends his holidays there regularly.
4. Did you like the group's last CD? You'll love this one!
5. You don't know Alice? Weren't you at my party last year?
6. He emigrated to Australia when he was a boy. He is a wealthy farmer now.
7. She learned to speak Arabic when she was a girl. She is working in Beirut now.
8. You bought your mountain bike three years ago? You need a new one now!
9. How will you recognize him? You've never seen him before!
10. "Have they ever been there?" – "No, they don't know the place." – "That's logical! If ..."

8

Join the two halves of the sentences with "if" or "when".

1. We can have a break		you want to learn French.
2. She'll pass her exams		she could speak Spanish.
3. I might go to Venezuela		I have enough money.
4. You should talk to Jean		my dad pays my fare.
5. They could go to Spain	if when	he'll be arriving.
6. We can get married		they aren't too hard.
7. She'd get a better job		Mr Johnson went with them.
8. I have no idea		this exercise is over.
9. You'll remember him		you see him next.

Bedingungssätze

Je nach Wahrscheinlichkeit der Bedingungserfüllung gibt es drei Typen von Bedingungssätzen. Die Reihenfolge der beiden Satzhälften ist beliebig. Statt *if ... not* wird oft *unless* benutzt.

Typ I – leicht erfüllbare Bedingungen: 30 – 99% erfüllbar

Hauptsatz: *will* + Infinitiv	*if*-Nebensatz: *simple present*
I'**ll tell** you my secret	if you **promise** not to tell anyone else.
I **won't tell** you what it is!	Unless you **promise** to keep my secret,

Typ II – sehr schwer bzw. überhaupt nicht erfüllbare Bedingungen: 0 – 29% erfüllbar

Hauptsatz: *would* + Infinitiv	*if*-Nebensatz: *simple past*
Would you really **tell** me your secret	if I **promised** not to tell anyone else?
I **wouldn't ask** you to tell me it!	If I **didn't know** I could keep your secret,

Typ III – reines Wunschdenken, da vergangenheitsbezogen: überhaupt nicht erfüllbare Bedingungen

Hauptsatz: *would have* + *past participle*	**if**-Nebensatz: *past perfect*
I **would have come** to your party	if you **had asked** me.
you **wouldn't have known** about it anyway!	If John **hadn't told** you about our party,

Merke:

- In allen drei Bedingungssatztypen können *will, would* bzw. *would have* je nach Bedeutung durch andere modale Hilfsverben (*can, could, might have* etc.) ersetzt werden.
- Statt der *simple present-* und *simple past-*Formen in den *if*-Teilen bei Sätzen der Typen I und II sind auch *present progressive* und *past progressive* in jeweils passenden Zusammenhängen möglich:
  If you**'re** really **working** hard, you'll be able to pass the exam.
  If I **were learning** Italian now, I might go to Italy in summer.

- Es gibt auch „Mischformen" bei den Bedingungssätzen:
  If you **enjoyed** her first CD, you**'ll like** her new one. (Typ II und I)
  I **wouldn't be** able to speak French fluently, if I **hadn't been** in France last year. (Typ II und III)

Achtung: *if* und *when* nicht verwechseln!

Bedingungssätze im Deutschen werden mit *wenn*, im Englischen mit *if* eingeleitet. Ein Nebensatz mit *when* im Englischen stellt keine Bedingung, die erfüllt werden muss, bevor die Handlung im Hauptsatz erfolgen kann. Bei *when*-Sätzen handelt es sich nur um den Zeitpunkt.

Vergleiche:

I'll phone you **when** I get home.	I'll phone you **if** I get home before ten.
100% sicher, dass er anruft – es fragt sich nur, *wann* er nach Hause kommt.	Hier wird nur angerufen, wenn er vor zehn Uhr nach Hause kommt.

Die beiden Hälften dieser if-Sätze sind durcheinander gewürfelt worden. Kannst du sie einander richtig zuordnen? Vergiss bitte nicht den Punkt oder das Fragezeichen am Satzende!

1. If we decide to go to Britain,	even if you'd promised to look after it	
2. If you invited us to your house,	I wouldn't have had to phone him	
3. I can't write her a letter	if I knew her address	
4. I'd write her an e-mail	if you had listened to me	
5. Would you lend me your CD	if I promised to look after it	.
6. I wouldn't have lent you my bike	you'll love the others	?
7. You wouldn't be in trouble now	unless you give me her address	
8. If you have written to him,	we would certainly come to see you	
9. If you had written to him,	I won't have to phone him	
10. If you read her first book,	we will definitely visit you	

8 Die indirekte Rede

8.1 Befehle in der indirekten Rede

Direkte Rede	Indirekte Rede

1. Die Befehlsform in der direkten Rede wird in der indirekten Rede mit einem Infinitiv wiedergegeben. Es spielt keine Rolle, ob das Einführungsverb in einer Zeitform der Gegenwart oder der Vergangenheit steht:

"**Stop** talking!"	Our teacher often **tells** us **to stop** talking. Yesterday he **told** us **to stop** talking twice.
"**Don't talk**!"	He **has asked** us **not to talk** several times. I **asked** you **not to talk** five minutes ago!

2. Aufforderungsverstärkungen bzw. -abschwächungen *(For goodness sake …!, Please don't ….)* werden nicht in die indirekte Rede übernommen, sondern durch ein relativ kräftiges bzw. mildes Einführungsverb zum Ausdruck gebracht. Diese Verben reichen vom „Betteln" bis hin zum „Brüllen":

"**For goodness sake don't lose** your tickets!"	Our teacher **begged** us **not to lose** our tickets.
"**Please be** a bit quieter!"	He **requested / asked** us to be a bit quieter.
"**Be** prepared!"	She **warned / told** them **to be** prepared.
"***Do*** **shut** up, Chris!"	I **ordered** Chris **to shut** up.
"**Take** cover!!"	The sergeant **roared** at us **to take** cover.

3. Vergiss nicht, dass ein verneinter Befehl nicht immer mit *"Don't ..."* ausgedrückt wird:

"**Never leave** the door unlocked!"	She told us **never to leave** the door unlocked.
Direkte Rede	**Indirekte Rede**

4. Wenn es sich weniger um Befehle als um einen guten Rat handelt, sind *recommend* oder *advise* geeignete Einführungsverben:

"**Don't eat** the fish!"	She **advised/recommended** me **not to eat** the fish.
"**Try** this ice-cream!"	He **recommended** us **to try** the/ this ice-cream.

In fast allen Fällen muss die Person, an die der direkte Befehl gerichtet wird, in der indirekten Rede erwähnt werden.

1

Look at the pictures and tell the story. Use the simple past with a suitable introductory verb for each situation – "asked, begged, told, requested, warned", etc. Start like this:

1. Yesterday Kate's mother ... rice and a few other things.
2. Her little brother Tommy ... .
3. Kate agreed (= "OK ..."), but ... .
4. In the shop Kate ... .
5. Then Tommy ... an ice lolly, but Kate said no.
6. Tommy started to cry, but Kate ... .
7. After that, Kate ... .
8. But Tommy was angry and pulled one of the shelves over. The shopkeeper ... .
9. Then the shopkeeper ... .
10. Outside, Kate ... .

2

Make full sentences out of the following direct commands. Be careful! The "command" given in sentence 11 is not given by people.

Example: "Fasten your seat-belts, please."

The stewardess asked the passengers to fasten their seat-belts.

1. "Please stop talking!"
2. "Empty your pockets!"
3. "Abandon ship!"
4. "Follow that car!"
5. "Wash this T-shirt in lukewarm water only."
6. "Don't hit your sister!"
7. "Always look over your shoulder when reversing."
8. "Never come into the gym with street shoes!"
9. "Shut up and sit down!"
10. "Meet me at the station."
11. BUY RILEY MOTOR-CARS
12. "For goodness sake don't drive so fast!"
13. "Put up your hands and stand perfectly still!"
14. "Fire!"
15. "Do pay attention, please!"

8.2 Aussagen in der indirekten Rede

Aussagen in der indirekten Rede

1. Wird die indirekte Rede mit einem Verb im *simple present* bzw. *present perfect* eingeleitet, werden alle Zeitformen „unverschoben" übernommen:

"I **live** in London now, but I **lived** in York for three years. We **have been living** in England since I **was** three, so I **can** speak English like a native. But we **are** German, and we **will be returning** to Germany soon."

Dolmetscher: Miss Meier **says** (that) she **lives** in London now, but that she **lived** in York for three years. She and her family **have been living** in England since she **was** three, so she **can** speak English like a native. But they **are** German, and **will be returning** to Germany soon.

"Petra **doesn't like** Munich. She **moved** there because of her job. After she **had been living** there for a week she **wanted** to go home."

Frank **has** just **told** me that his girlfriend Petra **doesn't like** Munich. She **moved** there because of her job. After she **had been living** there for a week she **wanted** to go home.

2. Wird die indirekte Rede mit einem Verb im *simple past* bzw. *past perfect* eingeleitet, müssen alle Zeitformen der direkten Rede um eine Zeitform nach hinten in die Vergangenheit verschoben werden. Bei Zeitformen, die mit Hilfsverben gebildet werden, wird nur das Hilfsverb verschoben:

"I **live** in London now, but I **lived** in York for three years. We **have been living** in England since I **was** three, so I **can** speak English like a native. But we **are** German, and we **will be returning** to Germany soon."

Miss Meier **said** (that) she **lived** in London now, but that she **had lived** in York for three years. She went on to say that she and her family **had been living** in England since she **had been** three, so she **could** speak English like a native. But she explained that they **were** German, and **would be returning** to Germany soon.

"Petra **doesn't like** Munich. She **moved** there because of her job. After she **had been living** there for a week she **wanted** to go home."

After Frank **had told** me that his girlfriend Petra **didn't like** Munich and **had moved** there because of her job, I asked him what her plans were. He **said** that after she **had been living** in Munich for a week she **had wanted** to go home.

Die häufigsten Einführungsverben bei Aussagen sind z.B. *he said, she told me, they promised, I assured him, we complained that* usw.

3

a) Are you a good interpreter? Your young friend from Germany can understand some English but is very shy and can't speak much English yet, so you have to help him/her. Some of your friends want to know a bit about life in Germany. Translate your friend's answers. Start every sentence with "He/She says (that) …"

Example: "Where do you live?" – "In der Nähe von Dortmund."
"He/She says he/she lives near Dortmund."

1. "Do you live in a house or a flat?" – "In einer Wohnung."
2. "What sort of music do you like?" – "Techno."
3. "Have you got any brothers or sisters?" – "Zwei Brüder und eine Schwester."
4. "What are your hobbies?" – "Fußball und Skateboarding."
5. "Do you play football at school?" – "Nein, ich spiele in einem Fußballverein (= club) ."
6. "Do you still go to school on Saturdays?" – "Nein – nicht mehr."
7. "Have you ever been to America?" – "Nein – noch nicht."
8. "When did you start learning English?" – "Erst (= only) vor einem Jahr."
9. "Do you like it over here?" – "Ja!"
10. "When are you going back to Germany?" – "In zwei Wochen."
11. "What were you doing yesterday afternoon?" – "Ich spielte Fußball."
12. "Yes, I saw you in the park. Who was that girl with you?" – "Das ist die Elke. Sie kommt auch aus Dortmund. Sie kam zum Fußballplatz, nachdem sie ihre Hausaufgaben gemacht hatte."

b) Am nächsten Tag musst du berichten, was dein Freund gestern sagte. Nimm die Sätze aus dem a)-Teil, fange aber mit: "He/She said …" an.

Wenn du etwas wiedergibst, ist es oft, aber nicht immer, notwendig, Orts- und Zeitangaben zu ändern.

Beispiel: "I was here yesterday" = He said he had been there the previous day/the day before.

Die häufigsten Umstellungen sind:

Direct	**Indirect**	**Direct**	**Indirect**
"here"	there	"tomorrow"	the next/following day
"this"	that	"yesterday"	the previous day/ the day before
"these"	those		
"today"	that day	"next week/month/year"	the following week etc.
		"last week/month/year"	the previous week etc.
		"a year/month/week ago"	a year/month before

4

Report the following commands and statements to suit the times and places given. Make any other changes necessary.

Examples:
"Meet me **here tomorrow**." (Cardiff – Monday a.m.)
(Cardiff – Monday p.m.) He told me to meet him **here tomorrow**.
(London – Tuesday) He told me to meet him **there/in Cardiff today**.

"I will be flying **to London tomorrow**." (Berlin, Tuesday)
(Berlin, Wednesday a.m.) Yesterday she told me that she **would** be flying to London **today**.

1. "I'm staying here tonight." (Leeds, Sunday a.m.)
   a) (Leeds, Sunday p.m.) She said …
   b) (Leeds, Monday a.m.) She told me yesterday morning …
   c) (London, Tuesday) On Sunday she informed me that …
2. "I saw John in London yesterday." (York, Tuesday)
   a) (London, Wednesday) Peter told me …
   b) (York, Friday) Peter told me …
   c) (London, Tuesday) Peter rang me and said …
3. "Go to Ireland for your holiday next year!" (Bristol, 2000)
   a) (Ireland, 2001) A friend recommended me …
   b) (Bristol, 2000) John advised me …
   c) (London, 2002) I was advised …

Manchmal muss man eine Kombination von Befehlen und Aussagen in der indirekten Rede wiedergeben. Ist eine Warnung begründet, brauchst du ein Einführungsverb für den Befehl und *because* für die Aussage:

"Put that gun down! It's loaded."
= He told me to put the gun down **because** it was loaded.

Manchmal ist ein Befehl die Folge einer Situation oder Handlung. Dann kann man den Befehlsteil mit *so* einbinden:

Dad: "It's a special occasion." Mum: "Yes. Wear your best clothes."
= Dad said it was a special occasion, **so** Mum told us to wear our best clothes.

Oft ist aber keine Begründung vorhanden, und hier brauchst du zwei unterschiedliche Einführungsverben:

"Wake up! I've got a surprise for you."
= My mother told me to wake up and said that she had got a surprise for me.

Versuche, die Sätze in der folgenden Übung nach den vorgegebenen Mustern in die indirekte Rede zu setzen.

5

Say what happened. Use an introductory verb in the past tense:

Example: Friend: "Be quiet! I'm thinking!"
My friend told me to be quiet because he was thinking.

1. *Teacher:* "I have to go and see the headmaster. Take out your books and do the exercise on page 23."
2. *Mother:* "Give me your old jeans. I want to wash them."
3. *Brother:* "I lent you £2. Give it me back!"
4. *Sister:* "Take that T-shirt off! It's mine!"
5. *Friend:* "Have another biscuit. I've got plenty."
6. *Policeman:* "This road has been flooded. Follow the DIVERSION signs."
7. *Uncle:* "Come in and sit down. Have a cup of tea. I wasn't expecting you so early."
8. *Inspector:* "This ticket is only valid with a Young Person's Railcard. Show me your Railcard, please."
9. *Ex-boyfriend:* "Go home! I didn't invite you to my party!"
10. *Notice:* Avoid the last-minute rush. Post early for Christmas.

8.3 Fragen in der indirekten Rede

Fragen ohne Fragewort

Bei Fragen unterscheidet man allgemein zwischen Fragen mit oder ohne Fragewort (*Who? When? How?* usw.). So auch in der indirekten Rede. Hier geht es zunächst um Fragen ohne Fragewort.

1. Mit Frageverb *Do/Does – Did*
   "**Does** he **like** ice-cream?"
   She **asks** me **if** he **likes** ice-cream.
   She **asked** me **if** he **liked** ice-cream.
   "**Did** he **know** the answer?"
   She **wants** to know **if** he **knew** the answer.
   She **wanted** to know **if** he **had known** the answer.

Die Fragebildung mit *Do/Does – Did* wird durch *if/whether* ersetzt, wobei natürlich die entsprechenden Änderungen in Verbform (evtl. 3.-Person-s in der Gegenwart) und Zeitform *("Did she know" = … if she knew)* vorgenommen werden müssen. Die „Zeitenverschiebung" ist die gleiche wie bei Aussagesätzen.

2. Mit Hilfsverb
   "**May** I **open** a window?"
   I **asked** him **if / whether** I **might** open a window.
   "**Are** they **going** to the party? **Will** John **be** there, too?"
   She **asked if** they **were going** to the party and **if** John **would be** there.
   "**Have** you **come** by car? **Can** you **give** me a lift?"
   He **asked** me **if** I **had come** by car and **whether** I **could give** him a lift.
   "**Hadn't** we better phone for a doctor?"
   They **wondered whether** they **hadn't** better phone for a doctor.

Hier taucht das Frageverb in der entsprechenden Zeitform nach der Einleitung mit *if/whether* wieder auf. Die Umstellung Hilfsverb – Subjekt wird aufgehoben.

Signalwörter: *if, whether* (= ob)

if ist ganz neutral. Bei *whether* schwingt die Bedeutung „… oder vielleicht auch nicht" mit.

6

a) Put the two halves of the sentences together. Be careful with the tenses!

1. I want to know if	I knew the right answer.
2. She wanted to find out whether	she had seen his umbrella.
3. He asked me if	the hotel had a good garage.
4. Our teacher sometimes asks if	his parents knew where he was.
5. The man asked her whether	the water is warm enough for swimming.
6. My mother wants to know if	this exercise is difficult.
7. The driver inquired whether	their son had received their letter yet.
8. He wondered if	we do our homework on the bus.
9. They wanted to know if	you'll be staying for supper.
10. I wonder whether	she could get a bus to Chelsham.

b) First check that your answers are correct. Then reconstruct the actual questions.

Fragen mit Fragewort

Anstelle von if/whether als Einleitung, wird das Fragewort selbst wiederholt. Signalwörter: *Who, What, When, Where, Why, How, How much, How often,* etc.

1. Mit *Who/What* als Subjekt:
   "**Who knows** the answer?"
   Our teacher **wants to know who knows** the answer.
   Our teacher **wanted to know who knew** the answer.
   "**What lives** in trees and **is** dangerous?"
   He **asked** me **what lived** in trees and **was** dangerous, so I told him:
   "A crow with a gun."

   Wenn *Who/What* als Subjekt der Frage benutzt wird, gibt es kaum Änderungen. Es muss nur die entsprechende Zeitform benutzt werden.

2. Mit Fragewort + *do/does/did*:
   "**Where** do you **live**?"
   He **is asking** you **where** you **live**.
   She **asked** me **where** I **lived**.
   "**How much did** those jeans **cost**?"
   "I **want to know how much** your jeans **cost**!"
   My mother **wanted to know how much** my jeans **had cost**.
   "**Who(m) do** you **know** in London?"
   She **asked** me **who(m)** I **knew** in London.

   Do/does/did als fragebildendes Verb fällt weg. Die entsprechenden Zeitverschiebungen gelten.

3. Mit Fragewort + anderen Hilfsverben:
   "**Why can't** you **come**?"
   Why on earth **is** he **asking** me **why** I **can't come**?
   He **asked** me **why** I **couldn't come**.
   "**How much has** that man **told** you?"
   They **wanted to know how much** the man **had told** me.

   Das Hilfsverb wird in die für das Einführungsverb entsprechende Zeitform „verschoben".

7

Put these questions into indirect speech. Use the introductions given.

1. "Who left the front door open?!" – My father asked me …
2. "What on earth are you doing here?" – She wants to know …
3. "How much money have you got?" – His friend asked her …
4. "How many prisoners had escaped before the prison staff found the hole?" – The reporter requested information about …
5. "When did the football match take place?" – He wants to know …
6. "How soon can you repair my car?" – The motorist asked the mechanic …
7. "What's happened to John?" – Our youth leader wanted to know …
8. "How far is Reading from London?" – One of the tourists has just asked …
9. "Where do flies go in the winter?" – The child asked his mother …
10. "What did you do after you had left the hotel?" – The detective asked me …

8

Here is a mixed bag of commands, statements and questions. Put them into indirect speech. You may need different introductory verbs (if you have a question and a statement to report) or a change of verb for stylistic reasons. Always use introductory verbs in the simple past and the characters suggested in brackets.

Example: "Turn left here. My house is on the right." **(driving instructor – me)**
The driving instructor told me to turn left (here) and informed me / was informing me that his house was on the right.

1. "Wake up! What's the matter with you?" **(sergeant – soldier)**
2. "I love French wine. Pass me the bottle!" **(Ken – Peter)**
3. "Does Patrick like wine, too? Let's offer him some." **(Peter)**
4. "Pay attention! I have to tell you everything twice." **(wife – husband)**
5. "Come here, Robin! Where did you get those sausages? You're a bad dog!" **(Tania – her dog Robin)**
6. "Are you Janet Smith?" – "Yes" – "Good. Come in and sit down. Have a cigarette." **(manager of the firm – young lady)**
7. "I was surprised not to see you at Phil's party. Where were you last night? Tell me the truth." **(Angela – her boyfriend Derek)**
8. "Let's wait a few minutes longer. I've no idea where the others have got to. Do you think they're lost?" **(Oliver – me)**
9. "Stop! You've run over a hen! Why can't you drive more carefully?" **(driving instructor – my sister/brother)**
10. "Let's finish this exercise and have a break." – "A good idea." **(teacher – me)**

9

Read the following newspaper article and reconstruct the interviews. There are three complete dialogues, so try the interview with Sarah first. Check your answers in the Key. If you think you need more practice, put another of the dialogues back into direct speech. You might like to leave the second dialogue for some later date (before a class test on this grammar topic, for instance). Remember: Don't try to do too much at once! A little – and often – is the key to success with this book.

And now the bad news – drug addiction figures are up again

The latest figures from the Department of Health, published today, show that more young people are experimenting with the drug Ecstasy.
A report by Patrick McGoughlan.

The time: 3 a.m. on a Saturday night. The scene: a disco in South London. Techno music and ravers on the dance floor. Most of them have taken stimulants to give them extra energy and keep them awake. Many are on drugs: not cocaine or heroin but ecstasy – the pocket-money drug.

I ask Sarah, a young black girl, when she started to take ecstasy, and she tells me it was at a party. I asked her what had made her start and she replied that everyone else had been taking something, so she had felt a bit of an outsider. Then I asked her whether she had ever tried any other drugs. She smiled and said that a friend had offered her a joint the previous week, but that she had refused it. When I asked Sarah if she thought she would want to try stronger drugs now, she told me that ecstasy gave her all she needed.

3.45 a.m. – The noise is so loud that I have to go outside to talk to Darrel, who is a dealer. I ask him how long he has been selling drugs, and he tells me that he started while he was still at school. He went on to say that he had been selling ecstasy and other tablets for about three years now. I asked him whether he did not have a bad conscience about exploiting young people, but he denied it. He said he knew that the tablets he was selling were 'good quality stuff'. When I wanted to know how much these tablets cost, he said that depended on what each customer wanted. When I asked him what he meant, he told me that some of the kids liked to mix ecstasy with LSD and cocaine. In answer to my question whether he didn't think taking cocaine was the way into the hard drugs scene, Darrel said that perhaps it was. It was a risk the kids had to take.

7.45 a.m. – Sheila Tate, aged 17, is not home yet. Her mother no longer waits up for her, but she got up early this Sunday morning to tell me about her daughter's drug problems. I asked her how her daughter had got involved in drugs. Mrs Tate told me Sheila had begun with dance drugs like ecstasy. My next question was how old she had been when she had started, and I was shocked to hear that Sheila had only been fourteen. Mrs Tate told me that she and her husband had been horrified when Sheila had been brought home early one morning in an ambulance.

Then I asked Mrs Tate whether she had not been able to stop her as she had only been fourteen at the time. Mrs Tate told me that they had tried, but the attraction of drugs had been stronger. "All her friends were on drugs."

I asked her what had happened after that, and Mrs Tate told me how Sheila had gone from ecstasy and LSD to cocaine and heroin. She was having medical treatment at a drugs centre at the moment. Sheila's addiction had broken up her marriage. Her ex-husband, she said, still blamed her for what had happened to their only child.

1. Direkte → indirekte Befehle:

"Come with me!"	→ He asked/told/ordered us to **come / go** with him.
"Don't wait for me."	→ She asked/told me **not to wait** for her.

2. Direkte → indirekte Aussagen:

Bei **Einführungsverben im *simple present* bzw. *present perfect*** bleiben die Zeitformen der direkten Rede erhalten:

"We **live** in Scotland."	→ They say (that) they **live** in Scotland.
"We **have lived** here for 10 years."	→ They say (that) they **have lived** here for 10 years.
"We **lived** in Germany before that."	→ They say (that) they **lived** in Germany before that.

Bei **Einführungsverben im *simple past* bzw. (selten!) *past perfect*** werden die Zeitformen der direkten Rede um eine Zeitstufe nach hinten verschoben. Grund: mit einem Einführungsverb in der Vergangenheit (*he said, she told me, after they had said* usw.) wurde auch der Blickpunkt um eine Zeitstufe nach hinten verschoben:

"We **live** in Scotland."	→ They **told us** (that) they **lived** in Scotland.
"We **have lived** here for 10 years."	→ They **said** (that) they **had lived** here for 10 years.
"We **lived** in Germany before that."	→ They **explained** (that) they **had lived** in Germany before that.

3. Direkte → indirekte Fragen:

"Do you know Paul?"	→ I **wonder if / whether** you **know** Paul. → I **asked** him **if** he **knew** Paul.
"Where did you live?"	→ He**'s asking** me **where** I **lived**. → He **asked** me **where** I **had lived**.

4. Direkte → indirekte Vorschläge:

"Let's go to London."	→ He **suggests / suggested going / that we should go** to London.
"Why don't we invite Tom?"	→ She **suggests / suggested inviting** Tom.

Eine kurze tabellarische Darstellung der Verschiebungen:

direkte Rede	indirekte Rede: Einführungsverb im *simple present* oder *present perfect*		indirekte Rede: Einführungsverb im *simple past* (oder *past perfect*)
Vollverben:			
simple present	bleibt	→	simple past
present perfect	bleibt	→	past perfect
simple past	bleibt	→	past perfect
past perfect	bleibt	→	bleibt
Hilfsverben:			
am/is/are (…ing)	bleibt	→	was/were (…ing)
have/has (been…ing)	bleibt	→	had (been …ing)
was/were (…ing)	bleibt	→	had been (…ing)
had (been …ing)	bleibt	→	bleibt
will/would	bleibt	→	would
shall/should	bleibt	→	should
can/could	bleibt	→	could
may/might	bleibt	→	might
must	bleibt	→	had to
needn't	bleibt	→	didn't have to

Merke:
- Bei Vollverben können nach einem Einführungsverb in der Vergangenheit nur *simple past* oder *past perfect*-Formen vorkommen.
- Bei den *progressive forms*, Futur usw. verschiebt man nur das **Hilfsverb** nach obigem Muster.
- Bei der Umwandlung der direkten in die indirekte Rede sind häufig auch Orts- und/oder Zeitverschiebungen nötig:
  here → *there, tomorrow* → *the following day* etc.

Was sagten die Leute? Kannst du die ursprünglichen Aussagen „rekonstruieren"? Um dir die Aufgabe etwas zu erleichtern, geben wir dir in Satz 1, 6 und 7 den ersten Teil der Lösung vor.

There was a bank robbery in our town last week. I was in the bank at the time. It was all very exciting!

1. The bank robbers had guns. One of them told the people in the bank to put their hands up and not to move or they would shoot.

   "Put your hands up ______________________________________!

2. Then he said that nobody would get hurt if they did what they were told.

   ____

3. One of the robbers asked the manager where he kept the keys to the safe.

   "____?"

4. The manager replied that there was no money in the safe. He said it had already been collected.

   "____

5. He informed the robbers that a security van *(Geldtransporter)* had come at 9 o'clock that morning.

   ____."

Jetzt geht's weiter. Diesmal musst du die direkte Rede in die indirekte Rede setzen.

6. "Don't lie to us! We've been watching the bank all morning!"

   The bank robber told him ______________________________

   ____

7. "It's the truth! The van came to the back door of the bank."

   The manager insisted ______________________________

   ____

8. "I don't believe you! Open the safe anyway!

   ____

   ____

9. If you don't open the safe, we'll shoot you!"

   ____

   ____

10. "Go ahead! Do you know that the police are on their way here? I can hear their sirens at this very moment!"

    ____

    ____

So could the bank robbers. They rushed out of the bank in confusion, so quickly, in fact, that one of them fell and broke his leg. The other two got stuck in the revolving door *(Drehtür)*, so the police caught all three. Their guns were not loaded, either!

9 Partizipien – Gerundium – Infinitiv

On his way home from school he **stopped to think** about his girl-friend's strange behaviour.

On his way home from school he **stopped thinking** about his girl-friend's strange behaviour.

Wo liegt der Bedeutungsunterschied zwischen Infinitiv und Gerundium nach dem Verb *to stop*? Im ersten Fall macht er eine Pause, um über das merkwürdige Verhalten seiner Freundin nachzudenken, im zweiten hört er auf, sich darüber Gedanken zu machen.

Neben der korrekten Verwendung von Infinitiv und Gerundium üben wir in diesem Kapitel noch den Gebrauch der Partizipien.

9.1 Partizipien als Adjektive und zur Verkürzung von Relativsätzen

Partizipien als Adjektive

Active	Passive
Our room has **running** water. *Unser Zimmer hat **fließendes** Wasser.*	We like **baked** beans. *Wir essen gerne **gebackene** Bohnen.*
This book is **interesting.** *Dieses Buch ist **interessant**.*	I am **interested** in history. *Ich bin an Geschichte **interessiert**.*

Partizipien zur Verkürzung von Relativsätzen

Zur Verkürzung von Relativkonstruktionen werden Partizipien wie folgt verwendet:

Present participle	Past participle
ersetzt eine aktive Zeitform.	ersetzt eine passive Zeitform.
The girl **who is sitting** there is my sister.	The man **who was seen** near the station was the thief.

The girl **sitting** there is my sister.	The man **seen** near the station was the thief.
I picked up the book **which lay** on the table.	The building **which was painted** last week is the bus station.
I picked up the book **lying** on the table.	The building **painted** last week is the bus station.

1

Use the correct participle form of the word in italics to complete these sentences:

1. "What are your *interests*?" – "I'm … in pop music and American football. I think they're very … ."
2. "What *frightened* your friend?" – "He saw a ghost. It was a very … experience for him. He's always been … of the dark."
3. "How long do you *boil* your eggs?" – "That depends. If you leave them longer than three minutes in … water, you get hard-… eggs."
4. When we arrived the rain was *falling*. We couldn't sleep because of the sound of … rain, and the next morning the grass was covered with … leaves.
5. "Have you *booked* tickets for the rock concert yet? Last time you forgot and the concert was fully … ." – "I must go down to the …-office this afternoon."
6. "Examinations *terrify* me." – "You needn't be … of your end-of-term tests. There's nothing … about them!"
7. "Why are you *wearing* your oldest jeans? They look so old and … out!"

2

Read the following story and write down all the relative clauses (which have been) shortened in the above ways.

Dropping your aitches

When I was a boy many people living in London spoke English with a Cockney accent. Originally, Cockney was the dialect spoken by people born in the East End of London: within hearing distance of the church bells of St Mary-le-Bow (known by Londoners simply as Bow Bells). Foreigners – or even many other Britons – listening to a real Cockney sometimes have great difficulty in understanding what he or she is saying. One of the things which makes understanding Cockney difficult is that Cockneys often leave out the h at the beginning of words. A Cockney saying: "'ave you 'ad any 'elp with this exercise?" is really saying: "Have you had any help with this exercise?" Cockneys educated at grammar schools try to avoid this "dropping of aitches", but sometimes someone less well educated puts a missing aitch in front of a word where it is not needed, and the result is: "Have you had hany help with this hexercise?"

3

Use a participle construction to shorten the relative clauses in these sentences:

Example: The girl who lives next door met me in the street.

The girl living next door met me in the street.

1. "The man who is standing over there looks familiar." –
2. "Which man? The one who is wearing the long raincoat?" –
3. "No. The one who is dressed in those dirty old jeans and a pullover." –
4. "Yes. Isn't he the man who was wanted by the police for that bank robbery?" –
5. "Don't be silly, Anne! Doesn't he remind you of the man who lives in the flat upstairs?" –
6. "You mean Mr Phillips? He doesn't wear clothes like that! He works at that bank which is situated right opposite my office. I see him every day." –
7. "Not Mr Phillips! The other man – the one who was invited to Jane's party last week. What's his name?" –
8. "I don't know. I didn't go to her party. But I know who you mean. He looks a bit like one of the men who work at the Station Garage. Perhaps that's why he's dressed like that." –
9. "Can't you remember his name?" – "It's a Scottish name which begins with Mac." –
10. "McTavish? ... McDougall ... Macintosh?" – "No. What's the name of that chain of restaurants which sells hamburgers and things?" – "MacChicken? MacBacon?" – "No, I'm sure it's McNugget ... something like that ..." – "You're hopeless!"

4

Look at the pictures and say what is happening. You should use a participle to shorten your sentences.

Example: 1. The young man **smoking** a pipe is reading the paper.
or: The young man **reading** the paper is smoking a pipe.

Neben den beiden bisher geübten Funktionen spielen die Partizipien eine wichtige stilistische Rolle, besonders im geschriebenen Englisch. In der gesprochenen Sprache kann man zwei Hauptsätze durchaus mit *and* verbinden. Beim Schreiben kann man etwas mehr am Satzgefüge „feilen".

Vergleiche:
"We looked at the menu **and** found that the food was quite expensive."
Looking at the menu, we found that the food was quite expensive.

9.2 Partizipien zur Verkürzung anderer Satzarten

Englisch	**Deutsch**
1. Zwei Hauptsätze (beide Handlungen gleichzeitig): She looked at her watch **and** saw that it was late. **Looking** at her watch, she saw that it was late.	Sie schaute auf ihre Uhr und sah …
2. Nebensätze mit Zeitbestimmung (eine Handlung vor der anderen): **After** he **had had** a good meal, he felt better. **Having had** a good meal, he felt better.	**Nachdem** er … **gehabt hatte**, …
Manchmal muss du die Konjunktion beibehalten, um den Zeitbezug deutlich auszudrücken:	
While waiting for the bus, he read the paper.	**Während** er …
When told that the police knew where he was, he left town.	**Als** ihm **gesagt wurde**, …
After having had a good meal, he felt better.	**Nachdem** er … **gehabt hatte**, …
Until told by his friends, he had no idea that he snored.	**Bis** es ihm seine Freunde **sagten**, …
3. Nebensätze mit Begründung *(because, as, since)*	
As / Because he knew the answer, he put up his hand. **Knowing** the answer, he put up his hand.	**Da / Weil** er die Antwort wusste, …
Since she **didn't** wish to get involved, she … **Not wishing** to get involved, she said nothing.	**Da** sie **nicht** darin verwickelt werden wollte, …
4. Nebensätze mit Bedingungen *(if, unless)* oder (seltener) bei Einräumungen *(although, though)*:	
If the meat is kept in a fridge, it will stay fresh. The meat will stay fresh **if kept** in a fridge.	**Wenn** …
You must keep on walking **unless** you are told to stop. You must keep on walking **unless told** to stop.	**Wenn … nicht** …
Although we live here, we don't know the place well. **Though living** here we don't know the place well.	**Obwohl** wir hier wohnen, …

NICHT VERGESSEN! – Bedingung ist: gleiches Subjekt in beiden Sätzen!

5

Shorten the following sentences using participles, but only where possible! Beware of unrelated participles (Partizipien, die sich nicht auf das Satzsubjekt beziehen!). Change these sentences if you can think of a way to do so, or leave them unchanged.

1. I walked across the room and shut the door.
2. When we had listened to the new CD, we went out for a hamburger.
3. Because he did not know the way he asked a passer-by.
4. As she wanted to go to the cinema, her boyfriend changed his plans.
5. Unless they are taught English properly, they will not be able to get good jobs abroad.
6. When passengers leave the train, they should take all their luggage with them.
7. Stay calm if you are stopped by a policeman.
8. Though it is made in Korea, this car is still very good.
9. The headmaster walked into the room and we all stopped talking.
10. The headmaster walked into the room and sat down at the teacher's table.
11. She had no worries until they told her she had to leave the country within 48 hours.
12. John went to Oxford after he had got four A's in his A-levels.

6

Now put these pairs of sentences together using the above constructions. In sentences followed by (2), two sentences are possible – please give both.

1. He shut the door. He sat down.
2. I passed my driving test. I bought a car.
3. She sat in the bath. She read a newspaper. (2)
4. We didn't want to go. So we stayed at home.
5. I didn't learn French at school. I wasn't able to read the letter.
6. My friend fell asleep. He was watching TV.
7. She did not live in the area. She could not help me.
8. Our dog ran off. It had bitten the postman.
9. They were foreigners. So they had to learn English.
10. I walk to school. I learn ten English words on the way. (2)

9.3 Partizipien nach bestimmten Verben

Partizip nach bestimmten Verben?

Die Verwendung eines *past participle* nach Verben der Ruhe *(stand, remain, lie)* deutet auf Folgen einer vorhergehenden Handlung hin. Im Deutschen wird oft eine ähnliche Konstruktion verwendet:

Englisch	**Deutsch**
The old car **stood** there **covered** with a sheet.	… **stand** mit einem Laken **zugedeckt** da.
The milk bottle **lay** there **smashed** to pieces.	… **lag zerschmettert** dort.
We **remained seated** when the film had finished.	… **blieben sitzen**.

Die Verwendung eines *present participle* nach Verben der Ruhe *(sit, stand, remain, lie)* oder des Kommens und Gehens *(come, go)* deutet darauf hin, dass beide Handlungen gleichzeitig erfolgten. Im Deutschen wird oft das Partizip der Vergangenheit eingesetzt oder zwei Sätze mit „und" verbunden.

She **came running** up to me.	Sie **kam** auf mich **zugelaufen**.
I can't **stand** here **talking** all day!	… den ganzen Tag hier **stehen** und **schwatzen**.
The cat **sat** there **looking** at me.	… **saß** dort und **sah** mich an.

Auch einige Verben des Zeitverbringens *(spend time, waste time)* werden mit dem *present participle* verwendet. Im Deutschen wird hier oft ein *gerund* oder ein Substantiv benutzt:

She **spends** hours **cooking**.	… **bringt** Stunden **mit Kochen zu**.
They **wasted** a lot of time **looking for** a parking space.	… **vergeudeten** viel Zeit **beim Parkplatzsuchen / auf der Suche nach** …

Einige weitere Ausdrücke *(keep s.o. waiting/standing/working, stop/catch s.o. doing s.th.)* werden mit dem *present participle* verwendet.

Im Deutschen steht oft ein Infinitiv:

My boyfriend **kept** me **waiting**.	... **ließ** mich **warten**.
Their boss often **keeps** them **working** until after 6 p.m.	... **lässt** sie ... **arbeiten**.
He **caught** the boys **stealing** his apples.	... **erwischte** ... beim **Äpfel-klauen**.
The government **stopped** immi-grants **entering** the country illegally.	... **hinderte** illegale Einwande-rer **am Einreisen**.

7

Use the above constructions to make one sentence out of each of the following pairs:

Example: They stood outside the cinema. They waited for the doors to open.
They **stood** outside the cinema **waiting** for the doors to open.
or: They **stood waiting** for the cinema to open.

1. She just sat there. She watched TV.
2. The children went down to the beach. They ran.
3. The policemen just stood there. They waited for orders.
4. The food remained. Nobody had touched it.
5. He spends a lot of time in discos. He is a good dancer.
6. The farmer caught two campers. They camped in his field without permission.
7. They have wasted a lot of time. They play football at the weekends.
8. The sailor lay on the grass. He was drunk.
9. They sunbathed. They spent a lot of time doing it.
10. I can't stand here all day and wait for you!

Partizip oder Infinitiv ohne to nach bestimmten Verben?

Nach Verben der „sinnlichen Wahrnehmung" *(see, hear, watch, feel)* wird der Infinitiv **ohne *to*** benutzt, wenn die **ganze Handlung** gesehen, gehört, gefühlt – erlebt wird.

Das Partizip der Gegenwart wird benutzt, wenn nur **ein Teil der Handlung** beobachtet wird:

> I saw a strange man **standing** outside the house. Then I saw him **climb** in through the open window.
>
> We watched the Queen **arrive**. For a while we watched the other guests **arriving** but went home before the last guests came.
>
> I heard the front door **open**. Then I heard someone **walking** slowly up the stairs towards my bedroom …
>
> For a second they felt the earth **move**. Then, just as suddenly, the earthquake was over. But they could still feel themselves **shaking** with fear.

8

Look at the picture and use the switchboard to make ten sentences. Use each verb twice.

When I was in London last week, …

			driv(e)/ing up and down.
		the hot sun	speak(ing) German.
	saw	several people	wait(ing) …
	watched	a police siren	break(ing) the sound barrier.
… I	listened to	a jet plane	wail(ing) in the distance.
	heard	the traffic	warm(ing) the back of my neck.
	felt	a street musician	look(ing) at the shop windows.
		a hand	play(ing) in the Underground.
			touch(ing) my shoulder. It was …

… my good friend Bob, who had walked up behind me in the street.

9.4 Gerundium und Infinitiv

Das gerund

Das ***gerund*** kann eingesetzt werden:

1. als Subjekt oder Objekt eines Satzes:
   Skiing is fun. I love **skiing**.
   auch als erweitertes Subjekt bzw. Objekt:
   Collecting pop CDs is expensive. I prefer **borrowing them from my friends**.

2. nach Präpositionen:
   We are looking forward **to visiting** Britain again.
   He paid for his holiday **by selling** his motor-bike.
   Are you used **to sleeping** with the window open?
   His teacher accused him **of cheating** during his exams.
   He was fined **for being** drunk.

3. für kurze Verbote (aber ohne eigenes Objekt)
   No **smoking** in the cinema.
   No **cycling**. **but:** Do not leave bicycles in the passage.

4. nach bestimmten Verben und Redewendungen:
   Do you **feel like going** swimming?
   I **love / enjoy / hate / detest learning** English.
   We **kept on working** and **put off taking** a break until we had finished.
   Would you **mind closing** the window?

5. mit eigenem Sinnsubjekt nach bestimmten Verben:
   My mother loves listening to pop music but
   she hates **me listening** to loud music in bed late at night.
   I'm sick of **him playing** that awful music!
   Would you mind **me opening** the window for a minute?

In der formalen Sprache wird die Form mit Possessivbegleiter bevorzugt:

She said she was tired of **his playing** loud music at night.
Would you mind **my opening** the window for a minute?

Hier eine Auflistung der wichtigsten Verben und Ausdrücke, die mit dem gerund – häufig mit eigenem Sinnsubjekt – verwendet werden:
avoid, deny, can't stand *(= kann nicht ausstehen),* can't help *(= kann nicht umhin, …),* enjoy, excuse, forgive, imagine, involve, it's no use/good *(= hat keinen Zweck, …),* it's (not) worth *(= es lohnt sich (nicht), …),* miss, postpone (= put off), prevent, resist, risk, stop, suggest

9

Read the letter and list the "ing"-forms in the following three categories:

Gerund	**Present participle**	**Continuous form**
I like living …	a living museum	I've been living …

Dear Uncle Jack,
I've been living in Central London for almost a month now and I must say that I like living in the big city. London is a living museum! Sitting on the upper deck of a bus on my way to school the other day I could see over the high wooden fence surrounding a big building site. As well as building workers I could see students looking for Roman remains on the site. Working as an archaeologist must be fun. I wouldn't mind studying archaeology when I leave school.
I love walking around the streets of London after dark. The mist rising from the lakes in the parks. The atmosphere in the oldest streets which you can only reach by walking through narrow alleys and passageways … I never thought I would find myself writing about a big city like this. But after living in London for nearly four weeks I have got used to hearing the sound of traffic rolling through the city all day and most of the night. Waking up at night, I sometimes wish it were a bit quieter, but living near the centre of a town makes life so much more interesting, don't you think?
I must stop writing now and start doing my homework. I look forward to seeing you at Christmas.

Yours,
Helena

Die Schwierigkeit bei der richtigen Handhabung des englischen *gerund* liegt darin, dass im Deutschen meist eine andere Konstruktion (oft ein Infinitiv) benutzt wird, so dass man „gar nicht darauf kommt", das *gerund* zu gebrauchen. Deshalb packen wir das Problem in der nächsten Übung von der deutschen Warte aus an. Alle Redewendungen, die du brauchst, findest du auf Seite 116.

10

Translate the following sentences into English. Use gerund constructions.

1. Schwimmen ist eines meiner Hobbies.
2. Ich schwimme gern im Meer.
3. Ich gewöhnte mich bald daran, in Salzwasser zu schwimmen.
4. Im Hallenbad schwimmen ist nicht so schön.
5. Ich habe nichts dagegen, am Wochenende ins Freibad zu gehen.
6. Mein Bruder hat nichts dagegen, wenn ich ohne ihn gehe.
7. Alte Schallplatten sammeln ist sein Lieblingshobby.
8. Er finanziert sein Hobby dadurch, dass er Zeitungen austrägt.
9. Meine Mutter mag es nicht, wenn er die Zeitungen bei schlechtem Wetter austragen muss.
10. Sie freut sich darauf, dass er bald einen richtigen Job anfängt.

Gerund oder Infinitiv nach bestimmten Verben in unterschiedlicher Bedeutung

	mit gerund	mit Infinitiv
go	We often **go swimming.** (shopping, skiing, etc.) *Wir gehen oft schwimmen.*	We often **go** to our local cinema **to see** a good film. *Wir gehen oft …, um … zu sehen.*
go on	He **went on talking** about himself. *Er redete unentwegt über sich. (= hörte nicht auf)*	He **went on to talk** about his car. *Er erzählte anschließend von seinem Auto. (Themenwechsel)*
regret	I **regret telling** him about my discovery. *Ich bedaure es, ihn von meiner Entdeckung informiert zu haben. (DAMALS gesagt, JETZT bedauert)*	I **regret to tell** you that the train is over an hour late. *Es tut mir leid, Ihnen (jetzt) sagen zu müssen, … . (schlechte Nachricht kommt jetzt …)*

remember	I **remember going** home. Ich erinnere mich daran, dass ich nach Hause ging.	I **remembered to go** home. Ich dachte daran, nach Hause zu gehen.
stop	She **stopped smoking**. Sie hörte auf zu rauchen.	She **stopped to smoke**. Sie hielt an, um zu rauchen.

11

Put in the right form (gerund or infinitive) of the verb in brackets. Make sure you understand the context before you make your choice.

1. **(remember – live)** I was born in London. Sometimes I try … what … in the big city was like but I don't remember much about my early life.
2. **(move)** I only remember my family … to the small village where we live now.
3. **(ask)** Last week our class went on a school excursion to London. Before we left I remembered … my mother for our old address.
4. **(shop)** I had a couple of hours to spare while the others went … in Oxford Street.
5. **(find)** So I took the Underground to the Elephant and Castle. But I had trouble … 13, Weston Street. The house numbers ran from 1 to 11 and began again at 15. There was a small playground where house number 13 had been.
6. **(ask)** I tried … some kids in the playground, but they had not lived there very long.
7. **(talk)** Then I asked two women who had stopped … in the street. "Number 13, dear?" said one. "They say 13 is an unlucky number, don't they? The house was empty for years after the last family left."
8. **(talk – tell)** She stopped … for a moment while two small children walked past. Then she went on … me about the house. Things my parents had never told me.
9. **(leave)** Now I realize why they never regretted … 13, Weston Street, London SE1. Three people had been killed there in the 1960s.
10. **(live)** "Nobody wanted … there for a long time afterwards. In the end they pulled the house down. They say it was haunted."
11. **(mention)** She went on … various other changes in the area.
12. **(say)** She talked for so long that I regret … I lied to her. I said I was in a hurry to catch a train. I had heard enough.

Partizipien – Gerundium – Infinitiv

Present participle

Das englische *present participle* endet auf *-ing*. Es hat einen vorwiegend aktiven Charakter und entspricht dem deutschen Partizip Präsens auf *-end*. Es kann:

- als Adjektiv benutzt werden:
  A **smiling** waiter *(Kellner)* greeted us.
- einen Relativsatz verkürzen:
  The woman **waiting** at the station was my Aunt Susan.
  = The woman **who was waiting** at the station …
- andere Nebensätze verkürzen:
  While waiting for the bus, we talked about our friends.
  After phoning her I went out. (= **After I had phoned** her…)
  Before going downstairs, I took my shoes off.
  Knowing that someone was listening, … (= **Because I knew**…)
  Not wanting to annoy her, … (= **As / Since I didn't want** …)

Wichtig! Da das Subjekt des abgekürzten Satzteils verschwindet, muss es mit dem Subjekt im Hauptsatz identisch sein.

Das *present participle* kann nach bestimmten Verben auch andere Konstruktionen im Deutschen ersetzen:

- einen Infinitiv:

Sie **ließ** ihn **warten**.	She **kept** him **waiting**.

- ein Partizip der Vergangenheit:

Das Auto **kam herangeprescht**.	The car **came racing** on.

- ein Vollverb:

Sie **saß** nur da und **strickte**.	She only **sat** there **knitting**.

Past participle

Das englische *past participle* ist die dritte Verbform eurer „Lernreihen" *(to come – came – **come**)*. Es entspricht der deutschen Verbform mit *ge-* und hat einen vorwiegend **passiven** Charakter. Es kann:

- als Adjektiv benutzt werden:
  He bought a **used** car. *(ein **gebrauchtes** Auto)*
- einen Relativsatz verkürzen:
  The man **arrested** was taken to the police station.
  = The man **who was arrested** …

- einen *if*-Satz verkürzen:
  This bread will stay fresh if **eaten** within three days.
  = … if it **is eaten** within three days.
- andere Nebensätze verkürzen:
  When (he was) **asked** his opinion, he said nothing.
  Passengers should wait here until (they are) **called**.

Auch bei diesen Verkürzungsmöglichkeiten gilt die Bedingung:
Gleiches Subjekt in beiden Satzhälften!

The gerund

Auch das englische *gerund* endet auf *-ing*. Es wird viel häufiger als seine deutsche Entsprechung *(das Schwimmen)* benutzt. Das *gerund* kann verwendet werden:

- als Subjekt oder Objekt eines Satzes:
  Reading is my hobby. I enjoy **reading**.
- auch als erweitertes Subjekt oder Objekt:
  Listening to pop music is fun. I like **listening to jazz**, too.
- nach Präpositionen:
  She earns her living **by teaching English**.
  I'm used **to getting up** early. *(… früh **aufzustehen**)*
- für kurze Ge- und Verbote:
  No **waiting**. No **smoking**. **Cycling** permitted.
- nach bestimmten Redewendungen:
  It's no use waiting for her.
- mit eigenem Sinnsubjekt nach bestimmten Verben:
  I don't **like people watching** me swimming.
  *(Ich mag es nicht, wenn die Leute mir … **zusehen**)*

Die Bedeutung bestimmter Verben hängt davon ab, ob sie durch Infinitiv oder *gerund* ergänzt werden. Vergleiche:

I stopped **eating** chocolate.	Ich **hörte auf**, Schokolade zu essen.
I stopped **to eat** some chocolate.	Ich **hielt an**, um etwas Schokolade zu essen.
He tried **to stop** smoking.	Er versuchte, das Rauchen **aufzugeben**.
He tried using nicotine patches.	Er versuchte es mit der Verwendung von Nikotinpflastern.

1

Wähle die richtige Ergänzung, aber pass dabei auf! Es sind mehr Wörter vorhanden, als du brauchst, und einige davon werden gerne mit dem richtigen Lösungswort verwechselt!

interesting / interested **to read / reading** **played / playing**

frozen / freezing **laying / lying / laid** **to shop / shopping**

break / breaking **picking / picked** **to learn / learning** **open / opening**

1. My elder sister is a big, beefy *(muskulös)* 19-year old. She has always been ______________ in sport.
2. When she was at school she played hockey in the school team. ______________ hockey was one of her hobbies.
3. They even played in the middle of winter, when the ground was ______________!
4. I went into her bedroom one day and saw a magazine ______________ on the floor.
5. ______________ it up, I saw that it was a paragliding *(Drachenfliegen)* magazine.
6. "Hey, Sis!" I said in surprise. "You aren't thinking ______________ to paraglide, are you?"
7. "Why not?" she replied. "It's a great hobby. You spend all your time ______________ books!"
8. "But what will Mum and Dad say? They won't want to see you ______________ an arm or a leg – or your neck!"
9. Just then we heard the front door ______________.
10. It was our parents coming back from ______________.

    My sister looked angrily at me and said: "If you tell Mum and Dad anything about this, I'll break *your* neck!"

2

Welche Form ist korrekt: a, b oder c?

1. Are you … in UFOs?
   a) interest b) interesting c) interested
2. Last week I read a very … story in the newspaper.
   a) excitement b) excited c) exciting
3. One evening a girl … home from school saw a bright light in a field.
   a) walks b) walking c) walked
4. She saw a spaceship … in a corner of the field.
   a) parking b) parked c) having parked
5. She stopped … what was happening.
   a) seeing b) to seeing c) to see
6. After … for a few minutes, the girl suddenly
   a) waiting b) await c) waited
7. saw the door … .
   a) to open b) opened c) open
8. A little green man got out. … to frighten the girl, he did not move towards her.
   a) Not wanting b) Not wanted c) Not to want
9. "Would you mind … just one question?" he shouted across the field. "Is this Wimbledon Common?"
   a) me answering b) answering me c) to answer me
10. "No," the girl shouted back. "This is Alexandra Park." "Farewell, then!" shouted the little green man, and climbed back into the spaceship. The girl watched the spaceship … quickly away into the night sky. Perhaps she should have said yes.
    a) flown b) fly c) flies

10 Das Passiv

10.1 *Simple forms* im Passiv

Du brauchst das Passiv, wenn

1. der Täter unbekannt oder so gut wie unbekannt ist:
   Someone **has eaten** all the food. = All the food **has been eaten**.
2. das Objekt des Aktivsatzes wichtiger als der Täter ist:
   They **made** a big decision. = A big decision **was made**.
3. der Täter sogar verheimlicht werden soll:
   My boss **has** just **made** a terrible mistake!
   = A terrible mistake **has been made**.
4. Anweisungen durch Befehle, Schilder usw. gegeben werden.
   Vergleiche:
   PE Teacher: "You **must** not **wear** street shoes in the gym."
   Notice on door: Street shoes **must** not **be worn** in the gym.

Die einzelnen Formen des Passivs werden im Deutschen mit „werden", im Englischen dagegen mit *to be* gebildet. Du musst also zwischen einer Passivform und der identischen Konstruktion *to be* + Adjektiv unterscheiden (z. B. *I **was** pleas**ed***).

Vergleiche:

I **was** surprised to see her.	I **was surprised** by the rain.
= *Ich **war** überrascht, sie zu sehen.*	= *Ich **wurde** vom Regen **überrascht**.*

Und so sehen die entsprechenden Formen aus:

	Active	Passive
Simple present:	I **write** the letters but	the bills **are written** by my wife.
Simple past:	She **saw** me in town	but John **wasn't seen** by anyone.
Present perfect:	We **haven't sold** our car.	It **has been stolen**.
Past perfect:	They **had gone** and	all the food **had been eaten** when we arrived.
will-future:	Someone **will drive** you home.	You **will be driven** home.

Auxiliaries:	You **can trust** him but	his friend **can't be trusted**.
	You **shouldn't eat** raw meat	and all water **should be boiled**.
	Someone **may have written**	or he **may have been rung** up
Infinitive:	I want **to take** the dog out. –	He doesn't need **to be taken** out again tonight.

Aktivsätze ohne Objekt können nicht in Passivsätze „verwandelt" werden, weil das Wichtigste fehlt: ein Objekt, das zum Subjekt des neuen Passivsatzes werden kann. Der Satz *"She **fell** down"* z. B. muss so bleiben.

1

You are going on holiday to Malta, but this is your first holiday on your own and you are not always sure what you should do. But the people you ask are very willing to help you.

Example: On the plane to Malta:
You: Must I show my passport?
Friend: Yes, all passports **must be shown**.

1. *You:* Will someone meet us at the airport?
   Friend: Yes, I expect ...
2. *You:* And must we open our luggage?
   Friend: Well, usually one or two pieces of luggage ... But it's only a formality.
3. *You:* Did your friend Mike book hotel rooms for us?
   Friend: Of course! Our ... weeks ago!

At the airport:

4. *You:* What about our luggage? It's quite heavy. Can someone take it to the hotel?
   Friend: That's no problem. Your luggage ... to the hotel, but I can carry mine.

In a souvenir shop:

5. *You:* Do the people on Malta make these souvenirs?
   Shop assistant: Oh yes, all our souvenirs ...
6. *You:* What about these stones? Did you pick them up on the beach?
   Shop assistant: No they ... in one of the caves.
7. *You:* Caves? *Shop assistant:* Yes. Malta is famous for its caves.

You: Do many tourists visit them? *Shop assistant:* Oh yes. The caves ... by thousands of tourists every year. Your hotel can arrange a visit.

At the hotel:

8. *You:* When can we take a coach trip round the island?
   Manager: ... on any morning of the week.
9. *You:* May we book two seats on this morning's coach?
   Manager: I'm sorry, but seats ... (not) ... in advance. Just wait outside the hotel. The coach won't be too full.
10. *You:* Have you arranged a trip to the caves for us?
    Manager: Yes. A trip ... for Thursday.

2

You are on holiday in Kenya with a friend. Your friend does not like the hotel – or the country – very much. In the following sentences you have to tactfully contradict what he or she says.

Example: "Yesterday someone **stole** my shoes." – "I'm sure they **weren't stolen**. I expect they wanted to polish them for you! Why don't you ask the manager?"

1. "Nobody **understands** English in this hotel!" – "That's not true. English ... by most of the people here." –
2. "I mean nobody in this country **speaks** *real* English!" – "So where ... ?" –
3. "In London, of course! People here **dislike** tourists." – "I don't think ... more here than in other countries." –
4. "And they're all thieves! Pickpockets **stole** the wallet of a friend of mine here last year." – "Well, my wallet ... in London last year." –
5. "And another thing. **Has** anyone **cleaned** your room yet?" – "Of course. My room ... every day so far. The maid comes in the morning.
6. After she **had made** my bed she asked me – in perfect English – if I would like her to clean the room." – "Hmm. When I told her that my bed ... n't ... since I arrived, she pretended she couldn't speak English." –
7. "That's strange! Maybe she just **doesn't like** you!" – "Perhaps you're right. I don't think ... by the people in Kenya!"

3

Sometimes people wish to divert attention from themselves. Look at the following police report of a peace demonstration in London. Who did these terrible things? In some cases, demonstrators, in other cases – nobody! Or at least that is what you might think when reading this report! Rewrite the report from the point of view of PEACE NOW magazine. Put the verbs in **bold type** into their active forms and put the real agents back into the sentences. Replace sentences where the agents are in **bold type** with passive sentences that hide their identities.

> Yesterday a forbidden demonstration in Trafalgar Square **was broken up**. A number of people **were arrested** when **violent demonstrators** injured several policemen. After **innocent bystanders** had called the police, about twenty policemen **were brought** to Trafalgar Square. The leader of the demonstration, the wellknown trouble-maker Jessica Davies, **was requested** to ask her fellow-demonstrators to go home, but she refused. **One or two demonstrators** were taken to Marlborough Street police station. Because they refused to give their names, they **were kept** there overnight. We **have not yet released** the ringleader of the rowdiest demonstration for several years. During the past few months four forbidden demonstrations **have been held**.

Write your article like this, and leave out negative words like "rowdy, forbidden", etc.

1. A heavily-armed police riot squad … a peaceful demonstration …
2. Angry policemen …
3. After the riot squad …, probably by unnamed police informers,
4. armour-plated police Land Rovers …
5. Bullying constables ordered Jessica Davies, the leader of the demonstration, …
6. Angry police armed with heavy sticks …
7. Catherine Binyon, chairperson of PEACE NOW, …
8. During the past few months our peaceful organization …

10.2 *Progressive forms* im Passiv

Es gibt im Passiv nur zwei gängige Verlaufsformen:

Active	**Passive**
Simple present progressive:	
They **are interviewing** him.	He **is being interviewed** right now.
Simple past progressive:	
They **were filming** the demonstration when we arrived.	The demonstration **was being filmed** when we arrived.

4

Look at the pictures and say what is – or is not – happening. You will need the progressive forms of the verbs above the pictures. The other words will help you.

industrial waste – to discharge 	rubbish – to dump 
private cars – not used efficiently 	valuable raw materials – throw away 

public transport – not used enough 	to build 
to close 	gas-guzzlers[1] – to develop 
not recycled 	cigarette advertising – not banned 

1 *gas-guzzler* = *Benzinschlucker*

5

A member of the Green Party is worried about pollution in his constituency[1]. He gives a short speech in Parliament, blaming the Government for many of the problems. A conservative newspaper reports his speech, but does not wish to mention the (Conservative) Government in its report. How would the reporter avoid mentioning the Government – or anybody else? Read the speech and write the report. You do not need to make the changes which are normally required for indirect speech.

"The present Government is doing nothing about air pollution. They are building two new by-passes[2] and another twenty miles of motorway in my constituency alone! Last year they promised to halt construction of a nuclear power station which they were planning, but they have done nothing, and a Government-sponsored company is already surveying[3] land near the River Don in preparation for construction of this power station which nobody wants! Big companies are still polluting the rivers in this beautiful part of Britain. Last year big companies were still expanding chemicals factories even though the Government had promised an enquiry into chemical pollution!"

1 *constituency* = Wahlkreis; 2 *by-pass* = Umgehungsstraße; 3 *to survey* = vermessen

10.3 Die Ergänzung durch *by/with*

Ergänzung durch *by/with/of* oder nicht?

Da das Passiv eingesetzt wird, wenn der eigentliche Täter unwichtig, unbekannt, selbstverständlich ist oder verschwiegen werden soll, ist eine Ergänzung des Passivsatzes mit *by* + Täter nur dann sinnvoll, wenn:

1. es sich um eine Änderung der Gewichtung Subjekt/Objekt handelt, keines von beiden aber so unwichtig ist, dass es ausgelassen werden darf.

   Vergleiche:
   Many people have welcomed the decision. (= not just me)
   The decision has been welcomed by most people.
   John Lennon wrote that song. (= not Paul McCartney)
   That song was written by John Lennon. (= not this song)

2. es sich um das Ergebnis einer schöpferischen Arbeit handelt. Der „Schöpfer" sollte erwähnt werden:

   The picture in the living room was painted **by Picasso**.
   This music was written **by a German pop singer**.

Ohne die Ergänzung wären solche Sätze unsinnig. Alle Musikstücke werden geschrieben, alle Gemälde wurden von jemandem gemalt. Wenn wir nicht wissen wollen, von wem das Lied geschrieben wurde, muss man solche Sätze wenigstens mit einer Orts-, Zeitangabe usw. ergänzen:

That photo was taken **in France during our last holiday**.
John's glasses were broken **in the playground yesterday**.

Wenn es sich nicht um einen Täter, sondern um ein Material usw. handelt, wird nicht *by*, sondern eine andere Präposition benutzt:

The house was filled **with smoke**.
The house was built **of stone**.

6

Make ten sentences from the switchboard using "by, with, of", etc. as necessary. Use at least four progressive forms.

1. This book 2. Thatched houses 3. Live music 4. Good sandwiches 5. Excellent fruit 6. Gas-guzzlers 7. The environment 8. Young people 9. Many souvenirs 10. Spanish	is/are (not) was/were (not) is/are (not) being was/were (not) being	spoken built polluted played made grown written trained banned sold	in … in Britain. of … with … by … on … as doctors. from … every year.

7

Be an editor. These are the headlines to twelve news stories which reporters working for your newspaper have written. But no matter what you think about these problems, try to be objective. You have to save space, too! So only add "by" … if necessary.

Perhaps you can find another way of expressing the agent if you need one (sentence 10).

1. Eco-crooks are dumping more industrial waste in our rivers than ever before
2. 10 photographers were following Prince William yesterday
3. The Nobel Committee has awarded the peace prize to a dog!
4. Fifth husband is divorcing famous film star
5. Teacher has been "selling" good marks to pupils for years
6. African dictator was spending foreign aid money on arms
7. Champion runner took drugs
8. 3 metres of snow are stopping traffic in northern Scotland
9. Hunters have been killing baby seals again
10. Pop star Madonna will cancel next concert
11. Man bites dog
12. Heavy rain is flooding many parts of Britain

10.4 Passivsätze mit Verb + Präposition

Verben, die mit Präposition + Objekt benutzt werden, werden wie folgt behandelt. Im Passivsatz steht die Präposition immer gleich hinter dem Verb:

Active	**Passive**
They throw the Coke cans **away** when they have finished **with** them.	The Coke cans are thrown **away** when they are finished **with**.
He is looking **into** the matter.	The matter is being looked **into**.
We must write **to** them at once.	They must be written **to** at once.
You should look new words **up**.	New words should be looked **up**.

Fragen zum Täter müssen durch *by* ergänzt werden:

Who wrote this book?	Who was this book written **by**?

8

One of the members of Duddington Rural District Council[1] is a member of the Green Party. At a council meeting last week he spoke about various problems. Other members of the council protested. What did they say? Be careful! You may need to change the tense in some cases.

1. The council is doing nothing about pollution! – That's wrong! Plenty … !
2. I disagree! Nobody is looking into the problem of recycling! – Rubbish! *(laughter)* The problem … at this very moment! An excellent local firm is already working out a new recycling concept. –
3. I don't care what … by your cousin's firm, June! We need action *now*! And what about road safety? When are we going to set up a traffic-free zone in the village? –
4. I think I can answer that. A traffic-free zone … as soon as we have enough money. And it's not just cars and lorries, Jonathan! Old Mrs Smith was knocked down by one of your Greens on a *bicycle* last week! –
5. But she wasn't badly injured. More people … and injured by motorists than by cyclists! –
6. Damned cyclists! They're a danger to pedestrians! If I had *my* way, I'd arrest them and lock them up for a few days! – And if I had my way, it's fast drivers like *you* who … !
7. Ladies and gentlemen – *please*! Let us move on to the next point: at the last meeting we were talking about bicycles obstructing the High Street. – You mean this matter … at a meeting where I was not present? –
8. I'm sorry, Jonathan. It wasn't on the agenda[2] sent out to all council members. Pauline brought it up – Pauline? – Yes, Jon, the matter … at the end of the meeting under "other business"[3].
9. There are bikes everywhere in the village now, thanks to you and your cycle shop, Jonathan! They are obstructing the pavements of the village streets. – I think the pavements … by all those cars! –
10. So we need a bigger car park. – It's not a bigger car park that … , Paul. It's fewer cars! –
11. We should tow away all those bikes! – Don't be ridiculous, Pauline! Bikes can't … ! You can *wheel* them away!
12. Not if they're chained up to lamp-posts! – But bikes have to … ! Otherwise people steal them. Thirty bikes … already this year! – Ladies and Gentlemen, *please*! It's almost midnight. We must turn our attention to the last point on the agenda: the proposed biological recycling plant on the edge of the village! – Ah!

1 *Rural District Council* = Gemeinderat; 2 *agenda* = Tagesordnung;
3 *"other business"* = Sonstiges

10.5 Passivsätze mit zwei Objekten

1. Bei Verben mit indirektem und direktem Objekt wird meist die Person (indirektes Objekt) zum Subjekt eines Passivsatzes:

   He promised **his daughter** an ice-cream.
   She was promised an ice-cream.

   The dictator promised **the people** free elections.
   The people were promised free elections.

   At first the government refused **me** a visa.
   At first **I** was refused a visa (by the government).

   The guide gives **each visitor** a brochure.
   Each visitor is given a brochure (by the guide).

Die wichtigsten Verben mit zwei Objekten sind:
to allow, to award, to bring, to deny, to give, to hand (= überreichen), *to leave, to offer, to promise, to refuse, to sell, to send, to show, to teach, to tell*

2. Bei den Verben, die das indirekte Objekt immer mit *to* anschließen, kann nur das direkte Objekt zum Subjekt des Passivsatzes werden:

   They explained the plan **to us** in great detail.
   The plan was explained to us in great detail. (**not:** We were …)

   Has my daughter introduced you **to the vicar**?
   Have **you** been introduced to the vicar?

Die wichtigsten Verben bei denen das indirekte Objekt immer mit *to* angeschlossen wird, sind:

to announce, to deliver, to demonstrate, to describe, to distribute, to explain, to introduce, to propose/suggest (= vorschlagen), *to say*

9

Make the indirect object the subject of a new sentence (where possible!).

Example: Someone brought him a cup of coffee and a cake.

He was brought a cup of coffee and a cake.

1. He handed me the note.
2. She has never offered me a ride in her car!
3. Didn't he send you an invitation to his party?
4. Haven't they taught you to say "please" if you want something?
5. They won't tell you the truth.
6. The Government is denying us our basic rights!
7. My doctor was giving me an injection when the lights went out.
8. The judges are going to award her first prize in the photographic competition.
9. No one has shown me the photos yet.
10. I didn't steal this bike. Someone sold it to me.
11. Her dad promised her a new skateboard for Christmas.
12. My great-grandfather has left me £5,000 in his will *(= Testament)*.

10

These sentences sound better if the direct object becomes the subject. Make any other changes that are necessary.

1. Someone delivered this parcel to the wrong address.
2. I can't explain this problem to people who know nothing about cricket.
3. Nobody has introduced them to the President yet.
4. One can only describe the scenery to you with the help of these photos.
5. I propose the following solution to you.
6. After the chemistry teacher had demonstrated the experiment to his pupils, the laboratory was full of smoke.
7. An official announced the results of the elections to the angry crowd.
8. No one said anything about this to me.
9. Helpers are distributing clothes to the refugees.
10. Someone suggested an alternative to the worried workers.

10.6 Unpersönliche Sätze und passivähnliche Konstruktionen

1. Wie bei den Verben mit zwei Objekten können unpersönliche Sätze manchmal verbessert – und im Englischen auch verkürzt – werden, wenn eine Person an den Satzanfang gerückt wird.
   Vergleiche die deutsche und englische Version des folgenden Beispiels:
   Es wird behauptet, dass er Nudeln mag.
   Von ihm wird (es) behauptet, dass er Nudeln mag.
   It is said that he likes noodles. *(unpersönlich)*
   They say that he likes noodles. *(schon besser!)*
   He is said **to like** noodles. *(die beste Lösung)*

   Im zweiten Satz ist der Täter unbekannt – ein typischer Fall fürs Passiv! Im dritten Satz hast du eine bekannte Person als Subjekt eingesetzt und den schwerfälligen Nebensatz mit *that* durch eine einfache Infinitiv + Objekt-Konstruktion ersetzt.

   Auch wenn ein Nebensatz mit *that* beibehalten werden muss, wird ein Satz mit persönlichem Subjekt vorgezogen:
   Someone told **us** that the plane was quite safe.
   We were told that **the plane** was quite safe.
   or: The plane **was said** to be quite safe.

   Diese Konstruktion ist nicht auf Lebewesen beschränkt, sondern kann überall eingesetzt werden, wo das Subjekt zu unbestimmt erscheint:
   People considered that **his plan** was crazy.
   His plan was considered **to be** crazy.

   Die wichtigsten Verben mit diesen Konstruktionen sind Verben des Denkens, Fühlens, Behauptens und Vermutens:
   to assume/suppose (= vermuten), *to believe, to claim* (= behaupten), *to consider, to feel, to find (= herausfinden), to know, to report, to say, to tell, to think, to understand*

   Da es sich um unsichere Behauptungen handelt, wird oft die Verlaufsform des Infinitivs *(to be + -ing)* verwendet.
   She was thought **to be living** in France. (= now)

Für Situationen in der Vergangenheit, die zum Zeitpunkt der Behauptung vielleicht nicht mehr zutreffen, brauchst du den *perfect infinitive*:
She was thought **to have been living** in France before she came to Germany.

2. Verben, die in der Aktivform durch einen Infinitiv ohne *to* ergänzt werden (besonders *see, hear, make* = lassen) müssen in Passivsätzen durch einen Infinitiv mit *to* ergänzt werden:

Someone heard him **leave**.	= He was heard **to leave**.
They often make me **wait**.	= I'm often made **to wait**.

Eine Ausnahme ist *let*:
The terrorists let their hostages **go** at midnight.
The hostages were let **go** at midnight.

11

After a bank robbery in London, one of the clerks who had been working in the bank when the robbers arrived tells her story. Rewrite what she says as a short newspaper report.

1. Our manager had told us that our bank was robbery-proof.
2. People said that the alarm system was perfect. But the robbers had no trouble getting in.
3. We now feel that the bank's security arrangements *(= Sicherheitsmaßnahmen)* were inadequate.
4. It is believed that the robbers had been hiding in the bank all night. They surprised us when we arrived for work.
5. They told us to put up our hands.
6. Then they made us lie down on the floor.
7. The police suppose that the gang is the same one that robbed the National Westminster Bank in Croydon last month.
8. Everybody knows that these men are dangerous criminals!
9. The robbers told us not to move for ten minutes
10. because they said there were other crooks outside, watching in case we gave the alarm.
11. People outside the bank saw the robbers leave in a fast car.
12. When they had gone we found that the manager, Mr Simms, had had a mild heart-attack!

Das Passiv

Formen des Passivs:

	Simple	Progressive
Present:	Dad's car **is made** in Britain.	Dad's car **is being repaired** at the moment.
Past:	The tyres **were checked** while	the car **was being repaired**.
Present perfect:	Dad's car **has** often **been repaired**.	–
Past perfect:	After it **had been repaired** he sold it.	–
will-future:	His new car **will be delivered** tomorrow.	–
Sonstige Hilfsverben:	It **must be paid** for in cash.	–
Infinitiv:	The tank only needs **to be filled** with petrol, then he can drive it home.	–

Es gibt also nur zwei Verlaufsformen des Passivs (*present* und *past*), die im Deutschen mit Wörtern wie *zur Zeit, gerade* umschrieben werden.

Verwendung des Passivs:

Sinnvoll wird das Passiv verwendet,

1. wenn der eigentliche „Täter" unbekannt oder unwichtiger als das Objekt des eigentlichen aktiven Satzes ist. Vergleiche:
   Someone stole my car yesterday. I have informed the police.
   My car **was stolen** yesterday. The police **have been informed**.
2. wenn der Täter, aus welchen Gründen auch immer, verheimlicht werden soll:
   My friend played a trick on our teacher.
   A trick **was played** on our teacher.

Eine **Ergänzung des Täters durch *by/ with*** etc. im Passivsatz ist nur sinnvoll,

- wenn er nicht so unwichtig ist, dass er weggelassen werden darf: We were attacked **by a gang of hooligans**. I was hit on the head **with a baseball bat**.
- bei schöpferischen Tätigkeiten, wo der „Schöpfer" natürlich erwähnt werden sollte: The Harry Potter books were written by **J.K. Rowling**.

Bei **Verben, die mit Präposition + Objekt benutzt werden** (*to talk to s.o., to look at s.th.* etc.) muss die Präposition gleich nach dem letzten Teil des Passivverbs kommen:

Aktiv: The police are looking into the matter at the moment.
Passiv: The matter **is being looked** into at the moment.

Bei **Aktivverben mit zwei Objekten** wird meist die Person (indirektes Objekt) zum Subjekt des Passivverbs, es sei denn, das indirekte Objekt (also die Person) wird mit *to* angeschlossen:

We were shown the plan and **it** was explained **to us** in great detail.

Schon wieder eine Klassenarbeit verhauen! Was ist bloß mit Melanie los? Hilf ihr doch mal. Aber Achtung: Drei Sätze hat sie richtig!

1. Morgan sports cars are still being made by hand in Malvern Link, a small town in England's Midlands.
2. The company has founded (to found = *gründen*) in the 1920s.
3. The first cars which produced were cheap three-wheelers. *(Dreiradfahrzeuge)*
4. They were thought to be safer than a motorbike with a sidecar. *(Beiwagen)*
5. One of the original three-wheelers was recently selling for £25,000!
6. Many of these old cars have been driving for hundreds of thousands of miles!
7. Today's Morgan sports cars are driven by all kinds of people.
8. Until recently, buyers have been invited to come to the factory at any time to see their cars while they were built.
9. But that tradition was thinking to hold up production. So it was stopping.
10. In future, buyers will asked to make an appointment before visiting the factory.

11 Modale Hilfsverben

11.1 Gebrauch und Formen modaler Hilfsverben

Modale Hilfsverben unterscheiden sich von anderen Verben dadurch, dass sie weder eine Handlung beschreiben (I **speak** English), noch – wie andere Hilfsverben – der Bildung einer Zeitform dienen (z. B. *to be/to have + -ing/-ed*). Vielmehr drücken sie eine Modalität in Zusammenhang mit einer Handlung aus:

I **can speak** English (*can* = Fähigkeit),
we **may go** swimming (*may* = Möglichkeit oder Erlaubnis),
she **must learn** (*must* = Notwendigkeit),
they **should drive** carefully, he **ought to drive** slowly
(*should/ought to* = Verpflichtung).

Formen

Modale Hilfsverben gibt es im Englischen in höchstens zwei Formen, wobei die zweite keineswegs dem *simple past* entspricht. Die Lücken füllen wir mit so genannten „Ersatzverben" *(substitutes)*. Es gibt weder eine Grundform zur Bildung der *will*-Zukunft noch Partizipien zur Bildung der Verlaufs- und Perfektformen.

1

Read the following brochure from the Action Group RETURN IMBER and make three lists. List One should contain all the modal auxiliaries in the text. List Two should contain all the substitutes (Ersatzformen) you can find. Put all the tense-forming auxiliaries in List Three.

Ministry of Defence

EVACUATION ORDER

Defence of the Realm Act – 15th October, 1943

NOTICE is hereby given that the Village of Imber in the County of Wiltshire is to be evacuated on 1st December 1943.

This Evacuation Order must be observed by all residents. Any persons who are not able to find accommodation in the area should apply to the Commanding Officer, Southern Command, Wilton, Wiltshire, who may be able to help.

Residents must take all their furniture and possessions with them, as no one will be allowed to return after the evacuation date.

From 2nd December 1943, all roads across this section of Salisbury Plain will be CLOSED TO THE GENERAL PUBLIC.

This Evacuation is for the duration of the War. Residents will be able to return to their homes as soon as the situation permits.

No exceptions can be made to this Order, which is issued in the interests of National Security

GOD SAVE THE KING!

It is now about 60 years since the last 150 residents of Imber, the most isolated village in southern England, had to leave their homes. They were allowed to take their possessions with them but were forbidden to return to the village even after the war.

The tiny village, of which only St Giles Church, Imber Court and a few half-ruined buildings have been allowed to remain, is situated right in the middle of Salisbury Plain – and in the middle of Army artillery ranges and battle-training areas.

The general public may only visit the village with the Army's permission on a few days every year, and people must not leave the roads to walk across the deserted meadows because they might be injured by unexploded ammunition from tanks and guns.

The action group RETURN IMBER believes that the Army ought to keep its promise and should return Imber to the people!

11.2 *Must* und *can / could*

must

Notwendigkeit

ich muss	I must	I have to
ich musste	—	I had to
ich habe gemusst	—	I have had to
ich werde müssen	—	I will have to
ich müsste	—	I would have to

Von *must*, das viel dringlicher klingt als *have to*, existiert nur eine Präsensform. Für die anderen Formen benutzt man *have to*.

Have to wird als Vollverb behandelt: Fragen und Verneinungen werden also wie gewohnt mit *do/does* – *did* gebildet.

"**Do** I **have to** eat this?" – "Yes, you **mustn't** leave anything!"
"**Did** she **have to** leave so early? Was it really necessary?"

In der Umgangssprache findest du aber auch Formen mit *got*:

Have we **got to** do our homework now?" = "**Do** we **have to** do …?

Vergiss nicht, dass „nicht müssen" im Englischen mit *needn't* ausgedrückt wird: *You **mustn't**!* ist ein Verbot, *You **must*** ein Gebot!

Must we go to the meeting? –
I'm afraid we **must**. But we **needn't** stay long.

can / could

Fähigkeit

ich kann	I can	I am able to
ich habe gekonnt	—	I have been able to
ich konnte	(I could)	I was able to
ich könnte	I could	I would be able to
ich werde können	—	I will be able to

Es gibt nur die zwei Formen *can* und *could*. ***Could*** kann nur in eindeutigen Kontexten mit klarem Vergangenheitsbezug mit „konnte" gleichgesetzt werden, weil es meist für die **Möglichkeitsform** steht.

Kontext eindeutig: **Could you? = Könnten Sie?**
Could you come quickly, doctor? – Of course. I **can** come now.

Could you? = Konnten Sie?
You went to the circus last night? **Could** you see everything? – Of course. We were sitting in the front row.

Kontext unklar: **Could** you go?
→ mit Ersatzform: **Were** you **able to** go?–No, we **weren't**.

2

Put in the right forms of "must", "have to" or "needn't":

1. "I'm a bit tired this evening. _______ we ___________ to go to Marilyn's party, Alan?" –
2. "We ________________ go if you're too tired. I'll ring her and say we can't come.
3. You've had a busy week. You ________________ overdo things." –
4. "No. I _________ to work very hard today and I ____________________ to work even harder next week." –
5. "Why?" – "Because our department ____________________ to move into new offices.
6. We __________________ to move three times in the last five years!" –
7. "Why ___________ you ___________ to move so many times?" –
8. "It's a long story." – "OK! You ________________ tell me if it's so long!" –
9. "You're right. I think I really ___________ go to bed now." – "Goodnight, Grandma!"

3

Put in the right form – or a substitute – of the verb used in the first half of the sentence.

1. "I **can't** help you today but I will ________________ help you tomorrow."
2. "Why **must** I help him? He _________ never _________ to help me!"
3. "Why **can't** you do your German homework this week?
   You ____________________ to do it all right last week."
4. "**Can** you explain the present perfect tense to me? I ___________ never ____________________ to understand when it is used!"
5. "John and Sandie **won't be able to** go on holiday until next month, but Claudia and I hope _____________________________ go next week."
6. "You'**ll have to** wait. The doctor ___________________________ see two other more serious cases first."
7. "**Have** you often **been able to** go gliding? – "Not often, but I want _____________________________ spend more time on my hobby next year."
8. "**Could** you help me?" – "If I had more time I ________________________ to help you."
9. "Why **can't** he tell you the answer?" – "He said he ____________________ __________________ find the book yet."
10. "I **haven't been able to** go skiing yet because I ______________________ __________________ find my ski boots."
11. "**Has** he **had to** leave school?" – "No, but he _________________________ work harder next year."

11.3 May / might

1. Erlaubnis

Darf ich?	May I?	Am I allowed to?
ich durfte	—	I was allowed to
ich habe gedurft	—	I have been allowed to
Ich werde dürfen	—	I will be allowed to
Dürfte ich?	Might I?	—

Die Frageform wird als Bitte um Erlaubnis verwendet. Die bejahte oder verneinte Form wird in der Beantwortung oder im üblichen Sinne von „dürfen" benutzt.

May I/we **watch** TV this evening? - You **may watch** TV until 11 o'clock but you **may not watch** any violent films!

Might wird in höflichen Fragen benutzt und steht für *may* in der indirekten Rede nach dem Einführungsverb in der Vergangenheit.

Die Antwort auf die höfliche Frage *Might we...?* etc. ist niemals *you might,* sondern fast immer das „großzügig" klingende *you may.*

Might I **ask** you a favour? - Of course you **may**!
May John **stay** the night? = He **asked** if John **might** stay the night.

Die Ersatzformen sind im Allgemeinen etwas schwächer im Ausdruck.

Dad says I **may** stay up later tonight. *(Sondererlaubnis)*
I **am allowed to** stay up until 11 o'clock most nights. *(generell)*

2. Möglichkeit

May und *might* können auch Unterschiede in der Wahrscheinlichkeit ausdrücken. *May* wird in dieser Bedeutung selten als Frage verwendet. In der Verneinung gibt der Kontext Aufschluss, ob es sich um eine Möglichkeit handelt (*He **may not** come.* = **Möglicherweise** kommt er nicht.) oder um die Verweigerung der Erlaubnis *(She **must** stay in bed. She **may not** get up.).* Im Deutschen wird *may* oft mit „können" oder „möglicherweise" übersetzt:

They **may** come if you invite them.
= **Möglicherweise** kommen sie ...
She **might** agree, but I don't think so.
= Sie **könnte evtl.** einverstanden sein ...

4

Put in the right form – or a substitute – of "may".

1. "He may be a good football player but he won't ... to play for us again unless he learns to play fair!"
2. "Might I ask whether I'll ... stay in Britain?"
3. "Caroline's mother says she may go to the cinema tonight but she (not) ... stay out later than 10 o'clock.
4. Please may I go, too, Mum?" – "No, you ..." –
5. – "Why not? Geoff ... go last week!"
6. The weather forecast said that it ... rain later.
7. "I don't know whether we ... go camping next month."
8. "... watch TV when you were a boy, Grandad?" –
9. "There was no TV when I was a boy, and we (not) ... waste time, either!"
10. "... I come in?" – "Of course."
11. "... I ask you exactly what your plans are?"
12. "If she went by plane she ... arrive in time."
13. "If you buy a lottery ticket you ... win £1,000." –
14. – "So if I bought ten lottery tickets I ... win £10,000?"
15. "I ... as well tell you that I'm too busy to see anyone at the moment."

5

What would you say in the following situations?

1. A good friend has a book that you would like to borrow. "...?"
2. You want to use your friend's father's computer. You have to be quite polite about it! "... possibly ...?"
3. You look closely at the £5 note. It looks like a forgery! You show it to your boss. "I think ..."
4. Is your friend too young to watch the horror video with you? Perhaps, but be tactful! "I think ..."
5. A holiday in Spain next year? It's very possible. "We ..."
6. A holiday on Hawaii? Less likely! "If we had more money ..."
7. Borrow my Rolls Royce? No! "You ...!"
8. Pop concert in Edinburgh next week? Alone? Your parents won't let you and your friend go. "I don't think we ..."
9. But if your big brother goes with you. "If my brother went with us I ..."
10. Abolish school uniform? Yes, your English friend is probably right. "You ..."
11. Abolish pocket money? You are not sure this is such a good idea. "It ..."
12. You are staying with your grandparents. They do not want to let you watch your favourite programme on TV. You protest: "At home I've always ...!"

11.4 *Shall / should*

Verpflichtung

Soll ich?	Shall I/we?	–
ich sollte	I should	I ought to
Sollten wir?	Should we?	Ought we to?
ich hätte sollen	I should have	I ought to have

Wie bei *may/might* sind die Frageformen relativ eindeutig. Bei verneinten Fragen wird meistens *should* verwendet.

Shall we go out into the garden?	= Sollen/Wollen wir ...?
Should we wait a little longer?	= Sollten wir ...?
Shouldn't they be here by now?	= Sollten sie nicht ...?

Bei *ought to* handelt es sich nicht um eine Ersatzform, denn dieses Verb füllt keine Lücken aus. Das Verb *ought to* drückt ebenfalls „sollten" aus.

Ought ist nur ein halbherziges Hilfsverb! Der darauf folgende Infinitiv braucht das *to* (wie bei *to want to: "I want to ask you a question"*), während eine Frage (s. oben) durch Umstellung (wie bei einem echten Hilfsverb) gebildet wird.

Für die anderen Bedeutungen von „sollen" gibt es im Englischen entsprechende Übersetzungen. Hierzu einige Beispiele:

1. „sollen" = es wird vermutet, behauptet

Jogging **soll** ungesund sein.	Jogging **is supposed / is said** to be bad for you.
Er **sollte** klug sein.	He **was said / supposed** to be clever.
Sie **soll** in London wohnen.	**They say** she lives in London.

2. „sollen" = es ist (meist von Dritten) angeordnet

Was **soll** ich tun?	What **shall** I do? *(Bitte um Rat)*
	What **am** I to do? *(verzweifelte Bitte)*
	What **am** I **supposed** to do? *(Was erwartest du von mir?)*
Wir **sollen** hier warten.	We **are supposed** to wait here.
	We **are** to wait here. *(strenger)*
Sie **sollten** entlassen werden.	They **were** to be fired. *(Vorhaben)*
Er sagte, ich **solle** in Zukunft vorsichtiger sein.	He said I **was** to be / **should** be more careful in future. *(indirekte Rede)*

3. „sollen“ = etwas ist festgelegt, vereinbart oder vom Schicksal verfügt worden

Er **sollte** am Montag kommen.	He **was (supposed)** to come on Monday.
Leider **sollte** der Komponist mit 33 Jahren jung sterben.	Unfortunately the composer **was** to die at the early age of 33.

4. „sollen“ = es wäre vielleicht gut/besser …

Wir **sollten** (lieber nicht) warten.	We**'d (= had) better** not wait.

6

An English-speaking friend is staying with you. What would you say to him/her in the following situations? Use the correct form of "shall/should, ought to" or one of the phrases to translate the German verb *sollen*.

1. Du schlägst eine Radtour aufs Land vor: "… a bike-ride in the country?" – "Fine!"
2. Es sieht nach Regen aus. "Perhaps we … rain capes with us." – "Good idea."
3. Trotzdem wäre es nicht gut, zu weit weg zu fahren. "Perhaps we … too far." – "You're right. Where shall we go?" –
4. Der kleine See am Waldesrand soll zum Baden gut sein. "The little lake on the edge of the forest …" – "OK. Let's go there."
5. Ihr radelt los. Bloß dein(e) Bekannte(r) fährt auf der linken Straßenseite los. Du schreist: "Hey! You … cycle on the left-hand side in Germany!"
6. "You're right! I … to know that by now!"
7. Ihr kommt am See an. Nach dem Baden zeigst du deiner/m Bekannten ein altes verfallenes Haus. Darin soll es spuken! "See that old house over there? … to be haunted." –
8. "Haunted? … have a look around?"
9. Gute Idee! Aber die Tür ist verschlossen, und es hängt ein Schild an der Tür: ZUTRITT VERBOTEN! "That sign means nobody … to go inside the house." –
10. "Perhaps we … go in, then."
11. Ja: wenn jemand euch sehen sollte, gäb's vielleicht Ärger. "Yes, if … we might get into trouble."
12. Jetzt ist's eigentlich Zeit, nach Hause zu fahren. "I think we … go home before it gets dark."

11.5 *Will / would*

1. **Bereitschaft, Wollen** (oft ohne Hilfsverb im Deutschen)

I'**ll talk** to Dad about it.	Ich **spreche** mit …
I've asked him to come but he **won't**.	… er **will** nicht.
Will you please be quiet!	**Wollen** Sie bitte …!
If you **will** just wait a moment …	Wenn Sie sich … gedulden **wollen**.

2. **Gewohnheit**

Will/would werden oft benutzt, um gegenwärtige oder ehemalige Gewohnheitshandlungen auszudrücken. Im Deutschen wird die Gewohnheitsmäßigkeit mit anderen Mitteln ausgedrückt:

Many London commuters **will** travel over 50 miles to work every day.	Viele Pendler fahren **regelmäßig**…
She **would** sit there for hours watching TV.	Sie **pflegte** stundenlang fernzusehen.
He **would** never listen to a word . I said	**Gewöhnlich wollte** er mir nie zuhören.

Ist die Gewohnheit lästig oder ärgerlich, wird das Hilfsverb (ähnlich wie bei *do/does – did* in Aussagesätzen) stark betont:

He ***will*** stay up late!	Er bleibt **doch immer** so lange auf!
She ***won't*** do as she's told!	Sie hört **nie** auf mich!
I ***did*** warn them, but they ***would*** try the food!	Ich warnte sie, aber sie **mussten / bestanden darauf** …
Boys ***will*** be boys!	Jungen sind **nun mal** so. (Sprichwort) = machen immer wieder dieselben Dummheiten!

Im Gegensatz zum „Gewohnheitsverb" *used to*, drückt *will/would* den „Willen" verstärkt aus. *Used to* ist neutraler:

I **used to** walk three miles to school each morning. *(= Gewohnheit)*
He **would** walk three miles to school in order to save his bus fare. *(= gewollte Sparmaßnahme in der Vergangenheit)*

Als Übersetzung für das deutsche Verb „wollen" kommen außerdem in Frage: *to want to* (Allzweckverb) / *to wish to* (stilistisch vornehmer) / *to desire to* (noch vornehmer als *wish*)

He **wants to** come with us.	Er **will** mit uns mitkommen.
Judge: "**Do** you **wish to** say anything in your defence?"	Richter: „**Möchten** Sie irgendetwas zu Ihrer Verteidigung sagen?"
The Queen **desires to** speak to you.	Die Königin **wünscht**, Sie zu sprechen.

to be willing to = bereit sein, gerne wollen

Are you **willing to** listen?	**Willst** du mir zuhören?
I'**m** quite **willing to** stay here.	Ich **will gerne** hier bleiben.

to intend to, to mean to = vorhaben, *to be going to* = die Absicht haben

The policeman asked her how long she **intended to** stay.	Der Polizist fragte sie, wie lange sie bleiben **wollte**.
I **meant to** ask her but I forgot.	Ich **wollte** sie fragen …
He **is going to** get married.	Er **will** heiraten.

would like to = möchten

What **would** you **like** to do?	Was **willst / möchtest** du machen?
I'**d like** to watch a video.	Ich **will / möchte** mir ein Video anschauen.

7

How would you translate these sentences? Don't just use "want" all the time. Pick the most suitable verb.

1. „**Wollen** Sie mit mir sprechen, Herr Direktor?" *(= Headmaster)* –
2. „Ach, Karin! Ja. Ich **wollte** dich heute Vormittag anrufen!" –
3. „Warum?" – „Ich **wollte** dich fragen, ob du am Klassenausflug teilnehmen **willst** (= möchtest) ." –
4. „Ich **wollte** eigentlich *(= really)* am Wochenende zu Hause bleiben.
5. Meine Tante **will** uns besuchen."
6. Sie **wollten** (= hatten die Absicht) den Film sehen, **wollten** aber nicht wegen Karten anstehen *(= to queue for)* .
7. „Was **wollen** (= vorhaben) Sie mit dem Geld tun?"
8. „Ich **will** (= Planung) ein Mountain Bike kaufen.
9. Ein Mountain Bike **habe** ich immer **haben wollen**."

Modale Hilfsverben

Die modalen Hilfsverben „helfen", die Handlung eines Verbs einzuschränken, indem sie ihr die „Modalität" der Notwendigkeit *(must)*, der Fähigkeit *(can, could)*, der Erlaubnis oder der Möglichkeit *(may, might)*, der Bereitschaft *(will, would)*, der Gewohnheit *(would)*, usw. hinzufügen:

Can you help me?	Kannst du mir helfen?
You **must** help me!	Du musst mir helfen!
We **mustn't** be late	Wir dürfen nicht zu spät kommen,
but we **needn't** rush.	aber wir müssen uns nicht beeilen.
You **should** be careful.	Du solltest vorsichtig sein.
You **ought to** know that.	Das solltest du wissen.
May I open the window? - No. -	Darf ich das Fenster öffnen? - Nein. -
Well **might** I take my pullover off,	Dürfte ich dann meinen Pulli aus-
then? It's very hot in here!	ziehen? Es ist sehr heiß hier drinnen!

Wie obiges Beispiel zeigt, ist bei den modalen Hilfsverben die zweite Form nicht die Vergangenheitsform, sondern die höflichere, ungewissere Form. Vergleiche:

Can you come?	Kannst du kommen?
Could your bring Bob?	Könntest du Bob mitbringen?

Das deutsche Verb *sollen* wird im Englischen nicht immer mit *shall / should* wiedergegeben:

sollen = Vermutung:	Sport soll gesund sein. Sport **is said / supposed** to be good for you.
sollen = Bitte um Rat:	Was soll(t)en wir (bloß) tun? What **are / were** we to do?
sollen = Verpflichtung:	Du sollst/solltest ruhig sein! You **are / were** (supposed) to be quiet!
sollen = Empfehlung:	Wir sollten hier warten. We **had better** wait here. (*natürlich auch:* We should wait here.)

Das modale Hilfsverb *will* wird meist zur Bildung des Futurs benutzt, hat aber auch die ursprüngliche Bedeutung des deutschen *wollen*:

Will you listen to me!	Willst/Wirst du mir wohl zuhören!
He **won't** do as he's told!	Er macht nicht das, was man ihm sagt!

Will und *would* werden oft benutzt, um gegenwärtige oder vergangene Gewohnheiten auszudrücken:
Some people **will** (= usually) do anything for money!
He **would** (= used to) spend hours playing with his model railway.

Was muss ich sonst über diese Verben wissen?

1. Mit Ausnahme von *ought to* wird der Infinitiv ***ohne to*** benutzt.
2. Die modalen Hilfsverben haben keine Verlaufsformen.
3. Um die Vergangenheit oder andere Zeitformen auszudrücken, musst du die entsprechende Form des Ersatzverbs *(substitute)* verwenden, z.B.:

Simple past:	I **had to** come.	Ich musste kommen.
Present perfect:	We**'ve been able to** stop.	Wir haben anhalten können.
Future:	They **won't be allowed**. to stay	Sie werden nicht bleiben dürfen.

Nicht vergessen:

You **mustn't** park here. = Du **darfst** hier **nicht** parken.
You **needn't** wait for me. = Du **musst nicht** auf mich warten.

Ergänze die folgenden Sätze mit dem am besten geeigneten Hilfsverb.

1. "Is it really necessary? ____________ we go to the school concert tonight? I'm very busy."
2. "It's not absolutely necessary. If you don't want to go, you ____________."
3. "But I can see you think that we both ____________ to go, don't you?"
4. "Well, I'm free tonight. I ____________ go alone if you're too busy."
5. "But we bought two tickets." –
   "Well, perhaps we ____________ bought two tickets if you're so busy."

Benutze ein Hilfsverb, um den Inhalt dieser etwas formal gefassten Sätze in die Umgangssprache zu bringen:

6. It is essential that you arrive on time.
   → You ____________.
7. Is it possible for me to talk to him now?
   → ____________ I ____________?
8. I have a very personal question to ask you.
   → ____________ I possibly ____________?
9. I really think it would be a good idea to stop here for the night.
   → We ____________ really ____________.
10. She used to watch TV until bedtime every night.
    → She ____________.

12 Relativsätze

12.1 Der Unterschied zwischen „bestimmenden“ und „nicht bestimmenden“ Relativsätzen

Bestimmende Relativsätze

Der „bestimmende“ Relativsatz *(defining relative clause)* vermittelt notwendige Informationen über eine Person oder eine Sache im Hauptsatz. Ohne diese Informationen wäre die Person oder die Sache nicht identifizierbar. Vergleiche:

Angela Barnes sits next to me in my class.	(Hier ist die Person namentlich genannt und somit deutlich identifiziert.)
The girl sits next to me in my class.	(Hier fehlt eine eindeutige Identifikation des Mädchens. Der Satz ist verwirrend, unklar.)
The girl who sits next to me is Angela Barnes.	(Mit dem *who* -Nebensatz ist das Mädchen eindeutig identifiziert.)

Ein bestimmender Relativsatz bildet sozusagen eine Einheit mit dem Begriff, den er beschreibt, und wird im Englischen ohne Pause angehängt. Ohne Pause bedeutet ohne Kommas, denn im Englischen ist das Komma immer ein „Pausenzeichen“.

Nicht bestimmende Relativsätze

Der „nicht bestimmende" Relativsatz *(non-defining relative clause)* gibt **zusätzliche Informationen** über eine Person oder eine Sache wieder, die nicht zur Identifikation der Person oder Sache notwendig sind.
Vergleiche:

The girl who lives next door is a good friend of mine.	(wird ohne Pause gesprochen)
That girl, who lives next door, is a good friend of mine.	(wird mit kurzen Pausen bei den Kommas gesprochen)

Es genügt ein Wörtchen wie *that*, im Gegensatz zu *the*, um eine Person deutlich zu identifizieren. Die Kommas funktionieren wie Klammern, zwischen denen in der Schriftsprache oft zusätzliche Informationen stehen.

Wenn wir die Kommas durch Klammern ersetzen, sehen die beiden Relativsatztypen so aus:

The old man who lives next door will be 93 next week.
John Wilkins (who lives next door) will be 93 next week.

In dieser Form ist die Funktion des Relativsatzes in beiden Sätzen klar.

1

Zuerst möchten wir dir abgewöhnen, immer zwischen Haupt- und Nebensatz – so auch in diesem Satz – ein Komma setzen. Das können wir natürlich nur mit bestimmenden Relativsätzen üben, wie:
A driver is a person ***who/that drives*** *a car, truck, taxi, bus* etc.
A screwdriver (Schraubenzieher) *is a tool* ***which / that drives*** *screws into wood.*

Verwende je nach Situation die Begriffe *person, tool, device* (Gerät), *thing* usw., um folgende Gegenstände zu definieren:

Beispiel: A mobile *(Handy)* is a telephone
which/that you can carry in your pocket.

1. A toaster is a device ____________________.
2. A winner is a ____________________.
3. Dinner is a meal ____________________.
4. A fridge is ____________________.
5. A bike is ____________________.
6. A manager is ____________________.
7. A wristwatch is ____________________.
8. Soap is ____________________.
9. Jam is ____________________.
10. Commas are ____________________.

2

Jetzt kannst du zeigen, ob du auch bestimmende und nicht bestimmende Relativsätze auseinander halten kannst. Vervollständige die folgenden Sätze mit sinnvollen Ergänzungen aus unten stehender Schalttafel. Manchmal handelt es sich um einen bestimmenden, manchmal um einen nicht bestimmenden Relativsatz.

			teaches us		
		who	is 16 years old		
…	,	which	were very expensive	,	…
		that	is in the garage		
			had red hair		

1. I saw the Harry Potter films first. Then Mum bought me all the books ______________________________.
2. He only bought cheap paperbacks. He didn't buy books ______________________________.
3. I have two sisters. This is a photo of my sister ______________________________.
4. My friend Harold ______________________________ lives in Bournemouth.
5. The woman ______________________________ French is OK,
6. but old Mr Strickland ______________________________ German is very strict.
7. Mum drives the car ______________________________.
8. My dad uses his old bike ______________________________, too.
9. My girlfriend ______________________________ lives next-door to me.
10. There's a girl ______________________________ in my class at school. She lives in your street, I think. Is she your girlfriend?

12.2 Die Relativpronomen als Subjekt und Objekt: *who / which / that*

Pronomen als Subjekt des Relativsatzes

Als Subjekt im Satz können folgende Relativpronomen verwendet werden.

Bestimmender Relativsatz:
who / that für Personen/Lebewesen:
The man **who / that** took the photo is my uncle.

which / that für Dinge:
The car **which / that** my mother drives is brand new.

Nicht bestimmender Relativsatz:
who für Personen/Lebewesen:
Doug Smith, **who** took the photo, is a friend of mine.

which für Dinge:
That old Fiat, **which** my father drives, is nearly 20 years old.

Das Relativpronomen *that* darf hier nicht verwendet werden.

Pronomen als Objekt des Relativsatzes

Hier gelten die gleichen Regeln wie für das Subjekt – nur, dass in der Schrift- bzw. gehobenen Sprache der Objektfall whom bei Personen benutzt wird.

Bestimmender Relativsatz:
The man **who(m) / that** I saw was very tall.

The girl **who(m) / that** I was talking to is only 15.

Nicht bestimmender Relativsatz:
The bank-robber, **who(m)** I only saw for a few seconds, was very tall.
Jennifer Jones, **who(m)** I was talking to when you arrived, is 15.

Ist das Relativpronomen Objekt im Relativsatz, so kann es – allerdings **nur** beim **bestimmenden** Relativsatz – sogar ganz weggelassen werden (so genannter *contact clause*).

The man I saw was very tall.
The girl I was talking to is only 15.

Nur in der gehobenen Schriftsprache findet man die im Deutschen noch übliche Fügung „Präposition + Relativpronomen“:

The man **to whom** I was talking is 84.	Der Mann, **mit dem** ich sprach, ist 84.

Nach Präpositionen ist die *whom*-Form obligatorisch.
Das Pronomen *that* darf nicht nach Präpositionen benutzt werden.

Viel häufiger – auch in der Schriftsprache – ist die Verbannung der Präposition ans Satzende.
Auch hier gilt: Ist das Relativpronomen **Objekt** im **bestimmenden** Relativsatz, kann es weggelassen werden *(contact clause)*. Diese Konstruktion wird in der gesprochenen Umgangssprache bevorzugt.

gehobene Schriftsprache:	The man **to whom** I was talking is 84.
normale Sprache:	The man who I was talking to is 84.
Umgangssprache:	The man I was talking to is 84.

Achtung:
Das Pronomen darf weggelassen werden, nicht aber die Präposition!

3

Aus zwei mach eins! Verbinde beide Sätze mit einem entsprechenden Relativpronomen. Manchmal kann man – wie in unserem Beispiel – das Objektpronomen im bestimmenden Relativsatz auch weglassen *(contact clause)*:

Beispiel: Have you finished the book? I lent you it last month!

Have you finished the book **which/that** I lent you last month?
oder: Have you finished the book I lent you last month?

1. Have you heard the CD? I lent it to your sister Caroline.
2. This is the boy. I saw him at the disco last week.
3. Here's my new bike. I got it for my birthday.
4. This is Linda. We talked to her at Jim's party.
5. They are the new group. You heard them on the radio yesterday evening.
6. John didn't see the car. The bank-robbers escaped in it.
7. We all know Mickey Mouse. Walt Disney invented him.
8. I like milk chocolate. You can buy it all over the world.
9. Have you read Petra's e-mail? She sent it two days ago.
10. You're the man. I've been waiting for you since lunchtime.
11. This is my bike. I left it in the garden overnight.
12. He wrote to a Scottish girl. He met her in Spain last month.

4

Setze das richtige Relativpronomen *(who/which/that)* in die Lücken ein. Auch ein paar Kommas (es sind wirklich nur ein paar!) musst du einsetzen! Versuche außerdem, so oft wie möglich das Relativpronomen auszulassen, wenn's geht:

Rugby is a game ____________ is extremely popular in Britain, France, Australia, South Africa, New Zealand and in fact many other Commonwealth countries(,) in ____________ the British way of life predominated (vorherrschte). The game was 'invented' by a boy ____________ was a pupil at Rugby School in 1823. He was the first player ____________, during a normal game of football, in ____________ players normally only kicked the ball, picked up the ball, ____________ in those days was not perfectly round but slightly oval, (as it still is in Rugby and American football today) and ran with it.

There are two types of Rugby: Rugby Union ____________ is an amateur sport played at schools(,) and Rugby League, a professional sport ____________ many people watch every Saturday in the North of England. There are fifteen players in a Rugby Union team and only thirteen in a Rugby League team. International Rugby matches ____________ the French and Welsh enjoy more than soccer matches(,) are played under Rugby Union rules and are well attended by thousands of fans ____________ often travel long distances to see the games.

The 'inventor' of the game, William Webb Ellis ____________ few people know by name(,) became a clergyman (Geistlicher) in later life, and died in 1872.

12.3 Das Relativpronomen im Genitivfall: *whose / of which*

Neben den Relativpronomen „der/die/das" usw. als Subjekt und Objektpronomen gibt es natürlich Relativsätze, die im Deutschen mit dem Genitivpronomen „dessen/deren" anfangen.
Im Englischen benutzt man sowohl im bestimmenden als auch im nicht bestimmenden Relativsatz das Pronomen *whose* bei Personen und *of which* bei Sachen.
Das Relativpronomen *whose* wird jedoch auch zunehmend in Bezug auf Sachen verwendet, um das nachgestellte, schwerfällige *of which* zu vermeiden.

Edison was an inventor **whose** ideas changed the world.	Edison war ein Erfinder, **dessen** Ideen die Welt veränderten.
J. K. Rowling, **whose** books almost everybody knows, invented Harry Potter.	J. K. Rowling, **deren** Bücher fast jeder kennt, erfand Harry Potter.
Basque, the origins of **which / whose** origins are unknown, is spoken in Spain.	Baskisch, **dessen** Ursprung unbekannt ist, wird in Spanien gesprochen.
Those are the shops **the windows of which / whose windows** were smashed.	Das sind die Läden, **deren** Fenster eingeschlagen wurden.

5

Bei den Genitivpronomen gelten natürlich auch die Kommaregeln für bestimmende und nicht bestimmende Relativsätze. Mal sehen, ob du die Kommas richtig setzen oder weglassen kannst!

Three students meet in the Hall of Residence *(Studentenwohnheim)* on the first day of term *(Semester – in GB eigentlich Trimester)*.

1. One of them is Kevin. His friend Günter has just arrived from Germany.
2. Günter is the German exchange student. His parents invited Kevin to stay during the summer vacation.

3. Kevin's best friend John is standing in front of the notice board in the corridor. Its notices are usually very interesting.
4. Kevin introduces his two friends to each other. "This is John. His parents are good friends of ours.
5. John, this is Günter, my German friend. I stayed with his parents during the summer vac (= vacation)."
6. "Hello, John. I'm the exchange student from Germany. My room is on the floor above yours."
7. "Pleased to meet you. Is that your car outside?" – "Which car?" – "The blue VW. Its windows are all open."
8. "Did I leave the windows open? It was so hot in town! I was stuck in a traffic jam behind a long line of cars. Their drivers all seemed to be asleep!
9. Should I go downstairs and shut the windows? Are there many car thieves on the campus?" – "Last term thieves stole several cars. Their owners had forgotten to lock them!"
10. "I'll go down and lock my car right away." But suddenly the three students heard a voice from a loudspeaker in the corridor: "Will the owner of the blue VW, German registration number HN-LS 317, please come downstairs at once. Your car's windows are open and the doors are not locked." – "Oops!" said Günter, and ran off down the corridor.

6

Diese Notizen sind für einen Zeitungsbericht bestimmt. Kannst du die Stichwörter mit entsprechenden Relativsätzen miteinander verbinden und den Artikel schreiben?

Old country *(ländlich)* railway station– Council *(Gemeinderat)* wanted to pull it down – saved at the last minute. The "Save our Station" campaign – leader Robin Wilson – talked to our reporter – said experts had examined part of the building – council had said the walls were unsafe – experts said the walls only needed a few simple repairs – any local builder could do them! – money (given by supporters of the campaign) almost enough for repairs – many people heard about the campaign – publicised by local radio stations: criticised the Council (Council's decision not widely publicised!) – Robin Wilson now looking for volunteers: come and help do the necessary repair work (it will take about four weeks) – chairman *(Vorsitzende/r)* of Council committee (he made the decision): very angry – Robin Wilson (local people admire him) – got married last week – met his wife (comes from London) as a result of his campaign work – both dynamic people – Council chairman dislikes them!

12.4 *Which* als satzbezügliches Pronomen

Which kennst du schon als Relativpronomen bei Sachen:

bestimmender Relativsatz: The book **which** I'm reading is by John Wain.
nicht bestimmender Relativsatz: This book, **which** cost me £10, is very interesting.

Eine weitere Funktion von *which* ist die Zusammenfassung eines vorangehenden Hauptsatzes im Sinne des deutschen „was" in Sätzen wie:

Sie trug einen Minirock, **den** ich sehr schön fand.	(Hier finde ich nur den Rock schön.)
Sie trug einen Minirock, **was** ich sehr schön fand.	(Hier finde ich die Aussage des ganzen Hauptsatzes - die Tatsache also, dass sie einen Minirock trug - schön.)
Der Zahnarzt zog zwei Zähne, **die** mir wehtaten.	(Die Zähne taten mir vorher weh.)
Der Zahnarzt zog zwei Zähne, **was** mir wehtat.	(Das Ziehen der Zähne tat mir weh.)

Jetzt das erste Satzpaar auf Englisch:

She was wearing a miniskirt *which* I thought was very nice.	(bestimmender Relativsatz)
She was wearing a miniskirt, **which** I thought was very nice.	(*which* in satzbezüglicher Funktion)

Das Relativpronomen *which* bezieht sich auf nur einen Begriff im vorhergehenden Satz. Das satzbezügliche **which** bezieht sich dagegen auf den ganzen vorhergehenden Satz.
Da sie nur einen Kommentar zum Hauptsatz abgeben, sind die mit dem satzbezüglichen *which* eingeleiteten Relativsätze immer **nicht bestimmend**. Wie alle nicht bestimmenden Relativsätze werden auch sie **mit Komma** vom Hauptsatz abgetrennt.

7

Benutze *which*, um aus folgenden Satzpaaren nur einen Satz zu machen. Vergiss dabei nicht das Komma!

Beispiel: I told him I had no money. This was perfectly true.
I told him I had no money, which was perfectly true.

1. She said she couldn't help me. It was just an excuse.
2. He arrived half an hour late. That was very impolite of him.
3. My sister watches TV a lot. Watching so much TV is not good for her.
4. Last week I went to a family wedding. I usually hate family weddings!
5. All my cousins were there. This made the wedding more fun.
6. Even my great-grandmother was there. This fact astonished everyone.
7. The old lady is 99 years old. Her great age makes her the oldest member of our family.
8. When my father saw my last school report, he got very angry. That didn't surprise me.
9. I had bad marks in most subjects. I couldn't explain this fact.
10. Luckily I had a 2 for English. This amazing result surprised my father.
11. He told me his best mark for English at school had been a 3. This shocked me.
12. What I didn't know was that his marks in other subjects had been bad too!

8

Welche Funktion hat *which* in folgenden Sätzen: satzbezüglich oder Relativpronomen im bestimmenden Relativsatz? Schreibe die Sätze mit der richtigen Kommastellung ab:

1. This is the book which I was telling you about. I read it in three days which is very fast for me! It's a story about a pop group which started up at our school.
2. Tom suggested a party which I thought was a good idea. Then Jenny suggested a barbecue which sounded like an even better idea. She said she had plenty of charcoal *(Holzkohle)* left from the barbecue which they had had last week.
3. He said he played the guitar in a pop group which was very good. His sister said that she was a singer in the same group which is nonsense. My friend John told me it was a true story which I didn't believe. But he has often told me stories which I didn't believe.

12.5 *What* als Relativpronomen

Im Gegensatz zum satzbezüglichen *which* als Entsprechung zum deutschen „was" wird die deutsche Konstruktion „(das,) was…" im Englischen mit *what* wiedergegeben:

(Das,) was er mir sagte, ist wahr.	**What** he told me is true.
Was du nicht weißt, ist, dass er oft lügt.	**What** you don't know is that he often tells lies.
Aber ich glaube immer **das, was** er mir erzählt.	But I always believe **what** he tells me.

Das englische Wort *what* wird also nicht nur in Fragen benutzt, sondern auch um ein Substantiv zu ersetzen oder zu erweitern, denn in unseren Beispielen könnte der erste Teil des Satzes durch ein Substantiv ersetzt werden:

What he told me is true.
= **His story** is true.

What you don't know is that he often tells lies.
= **The truth** is that he often tells lies.

But I always believe **what he tells me**.
= But I always believe **his stories**.

Besonders am Satzanfang und gelegentlich in der Satzmitte wird im Deutschen das einführende „das" oft weggelassen. Im Englischen brauchst du in solchen Sätzen immer nur das Pronomen *what*.

9

Benutze die *what*-Konstruktion als Ersatz für die fett gedruckten Satzteile. Benutze nicht die fett gedruckten Wörter, sondern ein geeignetes Verb deiner Wahl. Achte besonders auf die richtige Zeitform und auch auf die Tatsache, dass *what* als Singular aufgefasst wird:

Beispiel: I found it hard to understand **his wishes.**
I found it hard to understand what he wanted.

1. I find it hard to believe **his stories.**
2. **The thing that** is important is to learn ten new words a day.
3. Tell me something about **your mother's job.**
4. **His actions** were hard to explain.
5. I watched him carefully but couldn't observe **his actions** exactly.
6. **Their suggestions** were out of the question.
7. Three strong men are **necessary** to move this piano.
8. A big portion of fish and chips is precisely **my wish.**
9. **Your thoughts** are not important. **Your actions** are.
10. **The things that** go on at my school would surprise you!
11. "I've no idea **about his thoughts.**" – "**His thoughts** don't interest me! It's **his actions** that matter!"

Bestimmende und nicht bestimmende Relativsätze

Relativsätze liefern zusätzliche Informationen zu Personen oder Sachen im Hauptsatz. Diese Informationen können notwendiger (bestimmende Relativsätze) oder nicht notwendiger (nicht bestimmende Relativsätze) Art sein. Im Deutschen wird in der Schriftsprache kein Unterschied gemacht, da das deutsche Komma eine grammatische Funktion hat (Trennung von Haupt- und Nebensatz). Im Englischen wird der bestimmende Relativsatz „in einem Zug“ mit dem Wort, das er bestimmt, durchgesprochen, und da das englische Komma ein Pausenzeichen ist, wird in bestimmenden Relativsätzen aller Arten **kein Komma** benutzt.

Relativpronomen im Relativsatz

Relativpronomen	*bestimmender Relativsatz*
als Subjekt:	
Personen:	The girl **who / that** lives next door is nice.
Sachen:	The bike **which / that** belongs to me is new.
als Objekt:	
Personen:	The boy **(who / whom / that)** I like best is only 16.
Sachen:	The book **(which / that)** I read last week was good.
Genitivfall:	
Personen:	The girl **whose** eyes are blue is my friend.
Sachen:	The house **whose** garden is big is 80 years old.
	The house the garden **of which** is big is 80 years old.
Mit Präposition:	
Personen:	
Schriftsprache:	The boy **with whom** she arrived was very tall.
Umgangssprache:	The boy **(who / whom)** she arrived **with** was very tall.
Sachen:	
Schriftsprache:	The house **to which** we walked was small
Umgangssprache:	The house **(which)** we walked **to** was small.

Relativpronomen	*nicht bestimmender Relativsatz*
als Subjekt:	
Personen:	My girlfriend, **who** lives next door, is nice.
Sachen:	That bike, **which** belongs to me, is new.

als Objekt:

Personen:	Patrick, **who / whom** I like best, is only 16.
Sachen:	The book, **which** I read last week, is good.

Genitivfall:

Personen:	Your Diana, **whose** eyes are blue, is my friend.
Sachen:	Our house, **whose** garden is big, is 80 years old.
	Our house, the garden **of which** is big, is old.

Mit Präposition:

Personen:	
Schriftsprache:	Jim, **with whom** she arrived, was very tall.
Umgangssprache:	Jim, **who / whom** she arrived **with**, was very tall.

Sachen:	
Schriftsprache:	Tom's house, **to which** he walked, was small
Umgangssprache:	Tom's house, **which** we walked **to**, was small

Achtung:
- Das Relativpronomen *that* darf **nur** in **bestimmenden** Relativsätzen verwendet werden.
- Steht eine Präposition **vor** dem Pronomen bei Personen, ist die *whom*-Form erforderlich. Wird das Pronomen weggelassen, muss die Präposition auf jeden Fall bleiben.

Sonderfunktionen von *which* und *what*

Which kann sich auf den ganzen Inhalt des Hauptsatzes beziehen. In diesem Fall leitet es einen nicht bestimmenden Relativsatz ein – davor steht also immer ein Komma! – und hat die Funktion des deutschen Pronomens „was" (nicht „das" wie beim Relativsatz). Vergleiche:

They arrived in a sports car **which** I liked.	Sie kamen in einem Sportwagen an, **den** ich schön fand.
They arrived in a sports car, . **which** I liked	Sie kamen in einem Sportwagen an, **was** ich schön fand.

What entspricht dem Deutschen „(das,) was" – einer Fügung, die du nicht mit dem satzbezüglichen „was" verwechseln darfst!

What I have to say is very important.	**(Das,) was** ich zu sagen habe, ist sehr wichtig.
I don't know **what** you mean.	Ich weiß nicht, **was** du meinst.

Berichtige. Jeder Satz enthält mindestens einen Fehler, manchmal fehlt auch einfach nur ein Komma, oder es ist ein Komma fehl am Platz!

1. I read the book what you lent me.
2. It was the noise of the traffic, which kept her awake.
3. He asked me a question, that I couldn't answer.
4. He asked me a personal question, that was very rude *(unhöflich)* of him.
5. She is good at English which will help her in her new job.
6. We watched the rest of the match, whose first half we had missed.
7. Mike Summers about which I told you lives next door to us.
8. The friend, from who I got this letter, lives in Germany.
9. "Me? Angry? I don't know which you mean! I'm not angry!"
10. He suggested going swimming, what I thought was a good idea.
11. That what he said is probably true.
12. The Mr Brown, who lives in our street, is no relation to your Mr Brown.

Lösungen

1 Adjektiv und Adverb

1

a) Adverbs

1. with verbs:

goes **well** — will be lowered **gently** — flies **faster** than — can move as **fast** as — leap **vertically** — are **gradually** being explored — **easily** contain — will **far** outweigh — will benefit **immediately**

2. with adjectives:

equally great — **Majestically** moving

3. with other adverbs:

much more … than — **fairly** regularly

b) Adjectives

the **last** frontier — **next** year — a **revolutionary new** submarine — **first** voyage — **Deep** Flight I — **other deep-sea** research vessels — the … **highest** mountain — **manned** voyages … have become **common** — the **deepest** parts — **Deep** Flight I — are **most interested** in — the **deepest** parts — **little** is known about the **middle** waters — the … **last great** frontier — **more** life by weight — **other** ecosystem — their **economic** potential is equally **great** — **moving** ocean currents — **weather-related** disasters — **many valuable** minerals and **other** substances — discoveries **helpful** to

2

1. the Trieste was carefully lowered — 2. … two brave scientists. — 3. … behaved well — 4. … the complicated vehicles … contained only the passengers. — 5. They went down very slowly. — 6. They reached the bottom safely. — 7. … that men would soon be able … — 8. … increased dramatically. — 9. The old American … — 10. … vehicles remotely operated … followed quickly. — 11. … equipped with expensive cameras … — 12. … for scientific research. — 13. … marine biologists … — 14. A completely new era … — 15. … an imperfect basic knowledge … — 16. … an endless, flat plain stretching … — 17. … when closely examined … — 18. … astonishingly deep.

3

Across: 5. useful — 6. quickly — 8. unhappy — 9. far — 12. carefully — 14. first — 15. fully — *Down:* 1. slowly — 2. well — 3. quick — 4. loud — 7. sure — 10. full — 11. early — 13. awful

4

1. **good** snack-bar; really **well**; **better** than; the **best** place — 2. be **worse** than; the **worst** salads; doing **badly** — 3. **more interesting** than — 4. was **happy**; is **happier**

than; the **happiest** people; very **happy** — 5. find it **more difficult** than; it's **less difficult** than; the **most difficult** language — 6. have **much** time; had **more** time; as **much** money; **many** hobbies; **more** carefully — 7. have **less** time; has a **little** time; watches **less** than; watches the **least** of all — 8. feel **good** today; feel **better** than; would be **best**; work **better**; do **better**; did so **badly**; my **worst** exams; you'd **better**; won't do **well**; will be **worse** than — 9. **extreme** views; **extremely** strict; more **extreme** than; the **most extreme** headmaster

5

1. Adverb bzw. adverbiale Bestimmung am Satzanfang:
Sometimes there is high grass in a field — **Always** ask permission before you camp

2. Adverb bzw. adverbiale Bestimmung am Satz- oder Satzteilende:
it will be difficult for the farmer to cut the hay **later** — It is probably best to ask the farmer **first** — Dozens of sheep and lambs are killed **on British farms each year**

3. Adverb vor dem Vollverb (ohne Adverbien der Art und Weise):
you should **always** observe The Country Code — You should **never** walk across fields — Most paths are **clearly** marked. — Farmers don't **usually** mind — if you **thoughtlessly** walk across this field — Farmers will not **often** refuse permission — even though they **almost always** charge a small sum — Dogs **often** run after other animals — A strange dog will **certainly** frighten farm animals and may **possibly** injure them

4. Adverbien der Art und Weise:
Most paths are **clearly** marked. — if you **thoughtlessly** walk across this field — Follow them **carefully** — which a farmer has planted **specially** — their owners have not kept them **properly under control**

Folgendes Adverb passt nicht in eine der obigen Kategorien: unless you are **perfectly** sure (Adverb bestimmt Adjektiv)

6

1. We often go to bed at ten o'clock./At ten o'clock we often …
2. They have always lived in London.
3. Next year we are flying to Spain in the autumn.
4. Luckily he was not driving his car very fast.
5. She has never been to London in December.
6. I rarely watch TV at the weekends.
7. She only looked at it closely once./She only looked at it once closely.
8. Yesterday he nearly drove his new motor scooter into a wall./He … yesterday.
9. We regularly eat salad for lunch in summer./In summer we … for lunch.
10. Do you often come to the youth club on Fridays?

7

1. When we arrived at the campsite it was terribly late.
2. But we had often stayed at this site before, so that was no problem.
3. We put up our tent unbelievably quickly and were in our sleeping bags soon afterwards.
4. About an hour later I woke up./I woke up about an hour later.
5. I could hear someone walking quietly around the campsite.
6. My friend Tom was snoring loudly beside me.
7. He was a heavy sleeper.
8. Perhaps the warden was quickly making a last check / … was making a last quick check before going happily to his own bed.
9. Then I heard very quiet voices.
10. A man and a woman were talking softly to each other.
11. "This is an absolutely impossible place!" said the man.
12. "We can't possibly put up our tent here in the middle of the night. People are trying to sleep!"
13. "If we had left early and arrived here before midnight everything would have been OK.
14. Now we'll have to get up early and ask the warden if we can stay. It's all your fault."
15. "Why is it always my fault?" asked the man. "You're the one who is so terribly keen on camping!"
16. "Be quiet!" whispered the woman. "You'll wake someone up."
17. They didn't know that they had already woken me up./ … woken me up already.

8

Lösungsvorschlag:

1. The weather was very **bright** when we arrived in the Scottish Highlands. The sun was shining **brightly**.
2. We were very **happy**. We cycled **happily** along/through the countryside.
3. We cycled **carefully** down a steep hill./We were very **careful** because the hill was very steep.
4. It was still very **early** when we arrived at Loch Ness./When we arrived at Loch Ness it was still very **early**.
5. We felt very **lazy**, so we lay **lazily** on the bank of the lake/Loch Ness in the sunshine.
6. **Suddenly** Nessie, the Loch Ness Monster, appeared./We **suddenly** saw Nessie, the Loch Ness Monster.
7. **Quickly** I/I **quickly** picked up my camera.

8. Nessie was swimming **calmly** on the surface of the loch/lake.
9. We were very **excited**. We got on our bikes and cycled **excitedly** to the office of the Inverness News.
10. **Unluckily** there was no film in the camera!/**Unluckily** I had forgotten to put a film in the camera. We had been very **unlucky**! (= Wir hatten großes Pech gehabt.) We were very **unhappy** (nicht: unlucky) about our bad **luck**!

9

1. The CD sounded loud/terrible.
2. We looked carefully at the picture./… at the picture carefully.
3. She screamed terribly at the picture/when she saw my homework.
4. The explorers felt their way carefully along the tunnel.
5. Jackie gave a loud/terrible scream.
6. My teacher criticized me angrily/screamed terribly when she/he saw my homework.
7. The food smelt/tasted delicious/terrible/unusual.
8. The butler sounded the dinner gong loudly.
9. Her singing sounded beautiful/terrible.
10. I felt terrible after my flight. / I gave a terrible scream.

10

1. a high-flying aircraft — 2. a well-dressed girl — 3. a long-lasting battery — 4. a well-organized rock concert — 5. a badly-prepared lesson — 6. a sweet-smelling rose — 7. an attractive-looking girl — 8. a fast-moving vehicle — 9. a badly-scratched LP — 10. low-lying ground

Test

1. a) She is a **terribly** fast eater. b) correct
2. a) My friend John works more **slowly** than me. b) correct
3. a) correct b) That film was less interesting **than** I thought it would be.
4. a) I got **angrily** to my feet and walked out of the theatre. b) correct
5. a) Do you think that Melanie is **cleverer** than her brother? b) correct
6. a) correct b) Enjoy yourselves! I'll see you **at school on Monday**.
7. a) correct b) Have you **already** read her next book?
8. a) correct b) She worked **hard** for her exams.
9. a) He can't speak French but he speaks English **fluently**. oder: … **fluent** English b) correct
10. a) correct b) Your idea looks **good** on paper, too.

2 Zeitformen zur Wiedergabe von Gegenwart und Zukunft

1

1a), 2c), 3b), 4a), 5b), 6a)

2

1. My mother is not working in an office at present/at the moment. (Ort vor Zeit!) — 2. Oliver and Tanja play tennis every week. — 3. Do you always go to school at half past seven? — 4. He's always playing his violin! — 5. They are learning Spanish now/at the moment. — 6. He doesn't speak English well/good English. — 7. Does she never go swimming? — 8. I don't play football. — 9. He rarely listens to jazz. — 10. Next week I'm going to a rock concert. — 11. The last bus leaves at midnight.

3

Simple form:

The Channel coast … **has** some of the finest beaches *(kein Hilfsverb hier!)* — The White Cliffs of Dover **stand** guard — people who **want** to explore the countryside — Devon and Cornwall **lie** in the extreme south-west of England. — Visit Dartmoor and Exmoor, where ponies still **live** wild. — Cornwall **possesses** many interesting relics — (Cornwall) **is** still the home of china clay mining. *(kein Hilfsverb hier!)* — This **is** the Heart of England. *(kein Hilfsverb!)* — Every year many thousands of people **visit** the home of … — Tourists **love** the mellow stone houses — which they **find** in the Cotswolds. — places which **have** names like … — But the charm of the Cotswolds **does** not **end** with … — Visitors **come** from all over Europe … — Who **says** there is nothing to see … — … from the centre of Manchester **lies** some of England's prettiest moorland scenery. — It **runs** from Carlisle on the west coast to Newcastle … and **is** the biggest single national monument in Britain.

Progressive form:

If you **are planning** a holiday with a difference — … that **are waiting** to welcome you. — **Are** you **thinking** of spending longer than a week here? — Yorkshire … and its capital, York … **are waiting** to be discovered. — What **are** you **waiting** for? — We **are looking** forward to seeing you in England next year!

Modal auxiliaries:

You **can** explore the quiet country lanes in your own car. — Then you **might** like to rent one of the holiday flats — which **are to** be found in most of the larger towns. — Who **could** resist places which have names like …

4

1. aren't listening — 2. go; we are going — 3. They're having — 4. They have — 5. are they staying — 6. have — 7. take — 8. are driving — 9. are they coming — 10. Do you know — 11. don't think — 12. does she live? — 13. she's staying — 14. Do you mean; always arrives/ is always arriving — 15. believe; she's — 16. don't see — 17. are you; Do you like — 18. owes; need

5

Hier einige mögliche Ergänzungen:

Dear Penfriend,

My name is … and I live in …

1. At the moment I am writing to you!
2. I am fifteen years old/a fan of techno music.
3. Sometimes my family (and I) go out for a meal/go for a walk in the countryside.
4. Every week we/I visit our/my friends in …
5. We are usually at home on Sundays.
6. On Saturdays we never go to school/always go shopping.
7. I never forget to do my homework.
8. During the week we usually have lunch at home.

6

2. a) "**Are** you **going (to go)** to London next week?" — b) "(Please) **Will** you **buy** me a souvenir?
3. a) "**Shall** I **open** the window?" — b) "**Will** the noise of traffic **be** too loud?"
4. a) "**Aren't** you **going to offer** me a sweet?" b) "You**'ll have** a stomach-ache if you eat them all!"
5. a) "OK, I**'ll go**!" — b) "**Aren't** you **going to answer** the door?"

7

a) "I**'m** not **going to get** involved." — b) "I**'m** not **going to stop**." — c) "Nobody **will see** me if I walk away." — d) "Someone **will arrive** in a few minutes. I**'ll be** late for school if I wait any longer!" — e) "**Shall** I **call** a doctor?" — f) "Stay here! I**'m going to call** a doctor!" — g) "OK, I**'ll stay** here." — h) "I hope she **will be** OK." — i) "**Shall** we try and get her out?" — j) "I**'m** not **going to move** her." — k) "**Will** you **call** the police, too?" — l) "Yes, OK, I **won't be** long!"

8

1. Sue will be travelling to Birmingham. — 2. John will be ironing his shirts. — 3. Mum will be reading the paper. — 4. Dad will be sitting in the garden. — 5. Julia will be washing her hair. — 6. The boys will be playing football. — 7. Our teacher will be teaching (us) English. — 8. Pat and Jean will be listening to the radio. — 9. Our cat will be having (its) lunch.

9

1.+h) What will you do if you can't find the key? — **2.+e)** What will you be doing this time next week? — **3.+g)** Don't hit him or he'll tell the police! — **4.+b)** Don't disturb him because he'll probably be sleeping. — **5.+j)** Will they be having lunch when we arrive? — **6.+f)** Will they have lunch before we arrive? — **7.+i)** If we arrive late they will be having breakfast. — **8.+c)** When we arrive we will all have breakfast. — **9.+a)** She'll finish work at exactly ten past five. — **10.+d)** She'll be finishing work about now.

Andere Kombinationen sind auch möglich, so z. B.:

1.+f) What will you do before we arrive? —

2.+j) What will you be doing when we arrive?

Die alternativen Sätze bei 5 und 6 klingen allerdings dann etwas seltsam:

5.+e) Will they be having lunch this time next week?

6.+h) Will they have lunch if you can't find the key?

10

1. I will have passed my driving test. — 2. she will have finished her training. — 3. we will have been living/will have lived there for 10 years. — 4. will you have been learning English — 5. he'll have been talking — 6. He won't have been waiting — 7. he will have marked — 8. I'll have been saving — 9. I'll have saved enough — 10. Will they have arrived — 11. she will have been working — 12. she will have finished working — 13. they'll have finished building — 14. he'll have been studying English — 15. they'll have drunk

Test

1. Keep your eyes open for me at the station. I**'ll be standing** near the exit. — 2. At present my sister **is studying** English at university. — 3. Next year she **will have been** in Britain for five years already. — 4. My mother **works** in an office. She's a secretary. — 5. "When **will** I **see** you again?" — 6. "**Are** you **doing** anything on Friday evening?" – "No. Why?" — 7. – "I**'m giving** a party. Would you like to come?" – "Yes, of course! — 8. **Are** you **going to invite** Jean and Paul?" — 9. – "Yes. They**'re** always **complaining** that nobody invites them to parties, — 10. but I always **invite** them to mine!"

Das *past tense*: *simple* oder *progressive form*?

1

A light rain **was falling** when I **reached** the station. — It was while I **was looking** for a seat that I **saw** her. — ... and as I **was watching** I suddenly **saw** a young man ... — But the train **was travelling** quite fast now, so he **couldn't manage** to catch it. — Before five minutes **had passed**, Sheila and I **were talking** as if ... — By the time we **were passing** through York, I **knew** that I had found myself a new girlfriend. — I **looked** up ... and **saw** that Hilary **was walking** quickly ...

2

Background description:
I **was going** home after my first term at university, and I **was feeling** very happy.
I **was studying** in Edinburgh and still **living** with my parents
I **was** very much **looking** forward to going home
Many of my friends **were travelling** south on the same train,
The girl of my dreams **was sitting** there **reading** a paperback novel,
We **were** still **standing** at the platform.
Other young people **were putting** their bags ... between the seats
He **was running** after the train.
She **was facing** the other way.
She **was** not **smiling**.

was ...-ing = wollte
I **was keeping** this seat free for my boyfriend,
she **was staying** with an uncle and aunt over Christmas

One other progressive form is used. Did you write it down?
It is not a past progressive form, so don't worry if you didn't find it:
because my girlfriend Hilary **would be meeting** me at Kings Cross Station.

3

1.+g) She was talking to me when the phone rang. — 2.+j) Before the robber entered the bank, she put a mask on. — 3.+i) When we went on holiday, we always locked all the doors. — 4.+a) John talked to Sheila when they met at the pub. — 5.+h) First they bought the tickets, then they got on the train. — 6.+d) While we were playing tennis, all our clothes were stolen. — 7.+b) The boys grilled the meat while the girls were watching TV. — 8.+c) When I last saw the bank robber, she was wearing a mask. — 9.+e) They were on the platform when the train arrived. — 10.+f) The boys were grilling the meat when the dog stole the sausages.

4

1. waited — 2. were waiting — 3. did you say — 4. was talking — 5. was saying — 6. saw — 7. was doing — 8. was seeing — 9. talked — 10. did she do — 11. had — 12. was having

5

1. While I was walking to school one morning, I saw an accident.
2. Just as I was crossing the road, a car drove into/hit another car.
3. When the police arrived, the two drivers were arguing/shouting at each other.
4. While the two policemen were just getting out of their car, one of the drivers hit the other driver.
5. While the driver who had been hit was lying on the ground, the other driver ran off.
6. Just as he was running round the corner, he ran into/hit a passer-by, a fat man who was coming round the other way.
7. While the driver was getting up, one of the policemen caught him.

Test

1. "Hello, Hilary," I **said**.
2. I **wanted** to kiss her, but she wouldn't let me.
3. "Who was that girl you **were talking** to?" she asked.
4. "Girl? What girl?" I **was** still **hoping** that she hadn't seen us kissing.
5. "The girl on the train. You **looked** as if you were good friends!"
6. "Oh, you mean Sheila! She's an old friend of mine." – "Old enough to kiss like that?" – I **had** to think quickly:
7. "We're both in the university drama club. We're doing 'Brief Encounter' next term. There's a scene in the play where the hero says goodbye to the heroine at a station. We **were practising** the scene."
8. I could see she **didn**'t **believe** me.
9. She knew that I **was lying**.
10. I **was getting** really worried now. "Give me a kiss!" I said. "On one condition," said Hilary. "I want you to promise to send me a ticket for 'Brief Encounter'. I'd love to see the play with you two in it!"

Present perfect oder *simple past*? 4

1

1. Simple past – completed period of time is given or is clear from the context
Violent confrontations between police and Asian youths **provoked** widespread shock last weekend. The campaign **began** in Birmingham last year. When repeated complaints … **produced** no results, Asians **set up** vigilante groups to clean up the areas. The violent confrontation with police in Bradford last weekend **showed** that …

2. Present perfect – action still going on
Over the past few years Asians in Britain … **have felt** very worried … … there **have been** many cases of crimes … A sex magazine with photos of Asian girls **has been** in circulation for over a year, … *This display of "civic responsibility" **has**, however, **involved** Muslims in the criticism … that they are "anti-liberal". *Young Asians **have taken over** the … campaign … and **made** it more militant.

3. Present perfect – action (or actions) completed at an undefined time in the past
… the way in which the wider culture … **has invaded** the areas where they live. Drug-taking **has increased** within the Asian community, … All this … **has generated** a climate of moral panic. *Many Asians living in city centres **have found** that the value of their houses goes down … Muslims **have started** a campaign to protect themselves … *This **has led** to a conflict of values and ways of life. Many of them **have left** school without adequate qualifications, … … they **have adopted** Western values …

4. Present perfect – action takes place in the present or very close to the present
a gay magazine for Asians **has** just **appeared**

*Die mit * gekennzeichneten Sätze in den Abschnitten 2 und 3 könnten auch im jeweils anderen Abschnitt eingeordnet werden.*

2

Lösungsvorschläge:

play:
We played "hide and seek" as children. — I played "hide and seek" as a child. — Did you ever play "hide and seek" as a child? — Have you ever played football? — I/We often play football.

listen to:
Did you listen to the radio yesterday evening? — I/We listened to the radio yesterday evening. — We've/I've often listened to pop concerts on the radio. — I/We have never listened to pop concerts on the radio. — Have you ever listened to pop concerts on the radio?

visit:
Did you visit London last year? — We/I visited London last year. — Have you visited Frankfurt yet? — I/We have never visited Frankfurt. — We/I haven't visited Frankfurt yet.

eat:
Have you ever eaten fish and chips? — We/I have often eaten fish and chips. — Did you ever eat marmalade when you were in England? — I/We often ate marmalade when we were in England.

drink:
Did you ever drink beer when you were younger? — We/I never drank beer when we were/I was younger.

watch:
Did you watch a horror film on TV last night? — I watched a horror film on TV last night.

3

1. has gone; went — 2. have lived; lived — 3. Did you do; Have you done — 4. did not drive; have not driven — 5. learnt; have not learnt — 6. wrote; has written — 7. have bought; bought — 8. Have you often drunk; Did you often drink — 9. Has Julie ever flown; did she fly — 10. Have you seen; Did you see

4

1. We have seen this film twice. — 2. We saw this film last week. — 3. He lived/was living in Berlin when I knew him. — 4. My aunt works/is working in an office. — 5. My uncle has worked/has been working in England since 1990. — 6. Our teacher has visited/been to England three times. — 7. He has lived/has been living here for four years. — 8. He lived here for a year before he went/before going to the USA. — 9. She has just arrived. — 10. She always arrives punctually/on time.

5

… the White Tower, **was** built by William the Conqueror … **has been** used as a palace, a prison … Many people **have been** imprisoned or executed … including Anne Boleyn … who **was** beheaded here … Her ghost and many others **have been** seen

6

1. has always had — 2. was; was — 3. worked; did not live; preferred — 4. was built — 5. was called; have taken over — 6. ran; was

7

Jenny: Yes. I packed it yesterday. - Have you bought the food?

Paul: Yes/Of course. I bought it this afternoon. - (But) Have you packed your rucksack?

Jenny: I haven't finished (packing it) yet. I'm just doing/packing it.
or: Yes. I've just packed/finished packing it.
- Have you phoned the camp site (yet)?

Paul: Yes. I phoned them yesterday.

Test

1. "**Have** you **ever been** to Scotland?"
2. "Yes, I **was** there in **2001**. And you?"
3. "No, I**'ve/have never been** there.
4. But I**'ve/have just booked** an English course in Edinburgh.
5. I **saw** an advertisement for English courses in the newspaper a few days ago. 'English in Scotland' is the name of the company."
6. "Oh! I**'ve/have often seen** that advertisement.
7. A friend of mine **has already gone** on several 'English in Scotland' courses.
8. She **told** me all about them when I last saw her.
9. She **did**n't **seem** very happy about the accommodation.
10. but she **enjoyed** the courses very much."

5 Das *present perfect:* *simple* oder *progressive form*?

1

1. because I've been playing football. — 2. even though she has been living in London for three years already. — 3. How long have you been waiting here? — 4. I think someone has been drinking it! — 5. We've been practising English grammar since three o'clock. — 6. What has she been doing all afternoon? — 7. I've been looking forward to it all week! — 8. Has the baby been behaving well?

2

1. Have you learnt — 2. have you been learning — 3. I haven't seen — 4. John has been seeing — 5. They have been having — 6. They have never had — 7. she has been working — 8. You have worked — 9. have you been doing … I've been listening — 10. have you done — 11. Have you been watching — 12. They have been watching — 13. Have you ever been

3

Present perfect sentences:

1. John has been learning English / living here John has lived / has been working here	since last June.
2. We have been learning English / living here We have lived / have been working here	for three years/months.
3. She has been learning English / living here She has lived / has been working here	for six weeks.
4. They have been learning English / living here They have been working here	since they left Berlin.
5. Peter and Sophia have been learning English / living here Peter and Sofia have lived / have been working here	since three months / years ago.

Simple past sentences:

5. John/We/She/They/ Peter and Sophia came/lived here three months / years ago / for six weeks.

Other answers are also possible, but not simple past tense + "since"

4

1. For — 2. ago. — 3. since … since — 4. from — 5. Since — 6. For — 7. from — 8. ago — 9. since — 10. since

5

1. … even though this service **has been running for** fifty years.
2. They say that there has always been a bus service and that they have always used the buses. One woman says she has been using the bus since 1958
3. She is talking to some of the villagers. **"Have you written to the bus company?"** - "Yes, **but we haven't had/received a reply yet**."
4. "Well, **we have decided to take over the bus service (ourselves)**.
5. I **have worked/been working on the buses since 1994**." - "Yes. I think I'm a good driver because **I've had a/my driving licence for 9 years**.
6. and **I've never had an accident/I've not had an accident yet**."
7. "The villagers of Strathdon **have been discussing the problem for two and a half hours**.
8. A representative of the bus company **has just arrived**. I'll try and have a few words with him after the meeting."
9. "Well, not really. We **have had a frank and open exchange of views** but no real progress **has been made**.
10. The bus company **has decided to let them try for (a period of) three weeks**."

6

1. **Have** you **seen** my school-bag (anywhere)? — 2. **Have** you **been eating** my chocolate? — 3. Who **has eaten** (all) my chocolate? — 4. **Have** you **seen** Douglas Smith recently? — 5. **Have** you **been waiting** (for me) long? — 6. How long **has** he **been living** here? — 7. Where on earth **have** you **been**? — 8. What **have** you **done**? — 9. What on earth **have** you **been doing**? — 10. How long **have** you **been practising** English?

Test

1. I **haven't finished** my homework yet.
2. She **has been phoning** her boyfriend for half an hour.
3. We **have lived** here since 2001
4. *correct*
5. I **have been doing** my homework all afternoon. I need a break.
6. Our English teacher **started** at our school three years ago.
7. He **has** only **known** her for three days.
8. I met her two years **ago**.
9. *correct*
10. We **have known** them for three months.

6 Das *past perfect*

1

1. **After** Patricia **had passed** her driving test, she bought a car.
2. **After** she **had driven** home, she locked the car and went into the house.
3. **After** Patricia **had made** a cup of coffee, she phoned her friend Anna.
4. She put down the phone **after** she **had said** goodbye to Anna.
5. She looked out of the window **after** she **had heard** a loud noise.
6. Two young men were trying to steal her car radio **after** they **had broken** a window to get into the car.
7. **After** Patricia **had realized** what was happening, she rang the police.
8. Her neighbour came out of his house **after** he **had heard** the noise.
9. **After** the man **had shouted** something, the boys looked up and saw him.
10. **After** they **had run** away, a police car arrived outside Patricia's house.

2

1. **When** he told me his name, I knew who he was. — 2. **When** we **had** finished lunch, we went for a walk. — 3. **When** she **had** wiped her feet on the doormat, she shut the front door. — 4. **When** he took the dog for a walk, it was very cold outside. — 5. **When** our teacher **had** given us the dictation, he collected our exercise books. — 6. My mum learnt Russian **when** she went to school in East Germany. — 7. **When** the sun **had** set, the stars came out. — 8. I lit a match **when** the lights went out. — 9. **When** he tried to speak French, everybody laughed. — 10. **When** all my friends were on holiday, I felt very lonely.

3

1. After we **had flown** from London to New York, we booked into a hotel in Manhattan. — 2. After we **had been** on/**had taken** a sightseeing trip round Manhattan, we went to see the Statue of Liberty. — 3. After we **had celebrated** Independence Day in New York City, we went by car/drove to Washington. — 4. After/When we **had seen** the sights of Washington, we went/flew/drove to Disneyworld in Orlando, Florida. — 5. After/When we **had spent** two days in Florida, we flew to Arizona. — 6. After/When we **had visited** the Grand Canyon, we went to/visited Yosemite National Park. — 7. After/When we **had driven** over the Rockies to San Francisco, we stayed with friends there. — 8. After/When we **had seen** the Golden Gate Bridge and the other sights, we flew on to Seattle. — 9. After/When we **had spent** two days in Seattle with friends of Alan's, we flew back to London via Chicago. — 10. After/When we **had recovered** from the jet lag, we felt much better!

4

1. **Before** he **had finished** his lunch, his guests arrived. or: He (had) finished his lunch **before** his guests arrived. — 2. She bought a newspaper **before** the train left. — 3. We put warm clothes on **before** we went out into the snow. — 4. The boy jumped off **before** the bus **had stopped**. — 5. The TV programme started **before** we **had finished** our homework. or: **Before** the TV programme started, we finished our homework. — 6. We (had) reached home **before** it began to rain. — 7. **Before** they **had reached** the bus station, the bus left. — 8. She left school **before** she **had finished** her course. — 9. They left New York **before** they **had had** time to see the Statue of Liberty. — 10. **Before** we **had started** to eat, the others arrived.

5

Johnny Brown, the famous pop singer, was born in 1970. After he **had left** school in 1985, he started work as an assistant in a music shop. When he **had been learning** to play the guitar for three years, he joined the Steve Miller Band, which he left after he **had** only **been playing** for two months. After he **had been living** in New York for three years, he founded The Konks. When the group **had been playing** together for two years, it broke up. After he **had solved** his drug problem, he founded a new group The Daws. Their first concert was so successful that they could only leave the stage after they **had given** six encores. They made their first CD in 1994 after their fans **had been waiting/(had waited)** for two years! The group **had been working** together for three years when they broke up in 1996. They **had given** twenty concerts and made three CDs.

Test

1. He **had been waiting** at the station for two hours when the train finally arrived.
2. While he **was waiting**, he **read** a magazine.
3. He **was reading** an interesting article when the train **arrived**.
4. Ten minutes after the train **had left** the station, he **felt** hungry.
5. Because he **was feeling** hungry, he **left** his seat and went to the restaurant car.
6. After he **had had** a snack, he **walked/went** back to his seat.
7. As he **was walking** back to his seat, he **saw** a friend of his.
8. He **said** hello and **talked** to his friend for while.
9. When he **had been talking** to his friend for a few minutes,
10. he **remembered** that he **had left** his magazine in the restaurant car while he **had been having** his snack. So he **went/walked** back to look for it, but it was gone. Someone **had taken** it with him.

7 Bedingungssätze

1

1. I **will** visit New York. — 2. if you **invite** us. — 3. we**'ll have** the barbecue outside. — 4. unless we **pick** them **up** at the airport/**fetch** them from the airport. — 5. if I **give** it you back on Tuesday? — 6. you **will not/won't enjoy** this book. — 7. **Will** you **help** me … if I help you in the garden? — 8. if I**'ve saved** enough money by then. — 9. Unless you **call** the police, the robbers **will escape**! — 10. Unless we **run** faster, the bull **will catch** us!

2

1. may/might/can — 2. could — 3. could — 4. should — 5. may/might — 6. must/have to — 7. might — 8. needn't — 9. can — 10. mustn't/shouldn't

3

1.+e) — 2.+d) — 3.+a) — 4.+f) — 5.+b) — 6.+c) — 7.+i) — 8.+g) — 9.+j) — 10.+h)

4

1. will probably live — 2. knew — 3. is done — 4. Would … be — 5. will find — 6. were given — 7. will feel — 8. think — 9. are not/aren't trusted — 10. would … trust

5

Type I:

If you stand around a London Underground station for long enough you **will** probably **witness** at least one case of mugging.
If you **study** the few statistics available you **will find** that …
These … questions **will** still **have to be** answered if a solution to street crime **is** to be found.
Should you **try** to stop a mugging if you **see** one happening?

Type II:

But how **would** you **define** mugging if someone **asked** you …
If he **were** only **talking** about Central London, he **would** probably **be** right.
… in this area **would**, if **asked**, **describe** their attackers as "black".
… a mugging **would tend** not to be reported … **were** involved.

Type III:

If he **had thought** more carefully, … he **would not have caused** such a furore.

Others:

… a black **is** less likely to report … if he **is mugged** by another black
… if they **had been**, you **would** probably still **find** that mugging is …

6

2. If he had bought new tyres, he wouldn't have had a puncture. — 3. If he hadn't had a puncture, he wouldn't have got wet. — 4. If he hadn't got wet, he wouldn't have caught a cold. — 5. If he hadn't caught a cold, he wouldn't have moved into the Bed and Breakfast place. — 6. If he hadn't moved into the Bed and Breakfast place, he wouldn't have met Claire. — 7. If he hadn't met Claire, he wouldn't have climbed the hill. — 8. If he hadn't climbed the hill, he wouldn't have hurt his ankle. — 9. If he hadn't hurt his ankle, his holiday wouldn't have been spoilt.

7

1. If I **had won** a prize, I **wouldn't be** unhappy. — 2. John **wouldn't be living** in London now if he **hadn't found** a job there last year. — 3. If my friend **hadn't started** learning French a couple of years ago, he **wouldn't spend** his holidays there regularly. — 4. If you **liked** the group's last CD, you**'ll love** this one — 5. You **won't know** Alice if you **weren't** at my party last year. — 6. If he **hadn't emigrated** to Australia when he was a boy, he **wouldn't be** a wealthy farmer now. — 7. If she **hadn't learned** to speak Arabic when she was a girl, she **wouldn't be working** in Beirut now. — 8. If you **bought** your mountain bike three years ago, you **will need** a new one now! — 9. How **will** you **recognize** him if you**'ve** never **seen** him before? — 10. "If they **have** never **been** there, they **won't know** the place."

8

1. We can have a break when this exercise is over. — 2. She'll pass her exams if they aren't too hard. — 3. I might go to Venezuela if my dad pays my fare. — 4. You should talk to Jean if you want to learn French. — 5. They could go to Spain if Mr Johnson went with them. — 6. We can get married when I have enough money. — 7. She'd get a better job if she could speak Spanish. — 8. I have no idea when he'll be arriving. — 9. You'll remember him when you see him next.

Test

1. If we decide to go to Britain, we will definitely visit you.
2. If you invited us to your house, we would certainly come to see you.
3. I can't write her a letter unless you give me her address.
4. I'd write her an e-mail if I knew her address.
5. Would you lend me your CD if I promised to look after it?
6. I wouldn't have lent you my bike even if you'd promised to look after it.
7. You wouldn't be in trouble now if you had listened to me.
8. If you have written to him, I won't have to phone him.
9. If you had written to him, I wouldn't have had to phone him.
10. If you read her first book, you'll love the others.

8 Die indirekte Rede

1

1. Yesterday Kate's mother **asked her to go** to the shop and buy her a kilo of rice and a few other things.
2. Her little brother Tommy **begged her to take** him to the shop with her.
3. Kate agreed but **warned/told him not to ask** for any sweets.
4. In the shop Kate **told/warned Tommy not to touch** anything.
5. Then Tommy **wanted/asked Kate to buy him** an ice lolly, but Kate said no.
6. Tommy started to cry, but Kate **begged him not to cry** in the shop.
7. After that, Kate **told Tommy/her brother to wait** for her at the cash desk.
8. The shopkeeper **warned an old lady /shouted to an old lady to look out**.
9. Then the shopkeeper **asked/requested Kate to leave** his shop.
10. Outside, Kate **ordered/told Tommy never to do** that again.

2

1. The teacher/My mother/… asked us/me/… to stop talking.
2. The teacher/farmer/policeman/… ordered/told him/her/me/us/… to empty his/her/my/ our/… pockets.
3. The captain ordered/commanded the crew/passengers to abandon (the) ship.
4. The policeman/detective told/ordered the taxi-driver/motorist to follow that/ the bank-robbers' car.
5. The salesman/saleswoman advised/recommended the customer to wash this/ that/the T-shirt in lukewarm water only. or: … only to wash … water.
6. My/His/Her/The boy's mother/father told me/him/her not to hit my/his/her sister.
7. The driving instructor/teacher told/warned/advised his/her pupil to always look over his/ her shoulder when reversing.
8. The PE teacher warned/told the pupils never to come into the gym …
9. Our maths teacher/… ordered/shouted at/told us to shut up and sit down.
10. I/He/She/… asked him/her/me/… to meet me/him/her/… at the station.
11. The advertisement/poster recommended people/readers/passers-by to buy … .
12. He/She/I/… begged me/her/him/… not to drive so fast.
13. The policeman/bank-robber told/ordered the people/us/me/… to put up their/ our/my/… hands and (to) stand perfectly still.
14. The soldier/officer commanded/ordered the gunner/soldiers to fire.
15. Our teacher/… begged us to pay attention.

3

a) 1. He/She says he/she **lives** in a flat. – 2. He/She says he/she **likes** techno. – 3. He/She says he/she **has** got two brothers and a sister. – 4. He/She says his/her hobbies **are** football and skateboarding. – 5. He/She says he/she **plays** in a club. – 6. He/She says he/she **doesn't** go to school on Saturdays any more. – 7. He/She says he/she **hasn't been** to America yet. – 8. He/She says he/she only **started** English a year ago. – 9. He/She says he/she **likes** it over here. – 10. He/She says he/she **is** going back to Germany in two weeks. – 11. He/She says he/she **was** playing football. – 12. He/She says she/the girl **is** Elke and that she **comes** from Dortmund, too. He/She says she/Elke **came** to the park after she **had done** her homework.

b) 1. He/She said he/she **lived** in a flat. – 2. He/She said he/she **liked** techno. – 3. He/She said he/she **had** got two brothers and a sister. – 4. He/She said his/her hobbies **were** football and skateboarding. – 5. He/She said he/she **played** in a club. – 6. He/She said he/she **didn't** go to school on Saturdays any more. – 7. He/She said he/she **hadn't been** to America yet. – 8. He/She said he/she had only **started** English a year ago. – 9. He/She said he/she **liked** it over here. – 10. He/She said he/she **was** going back to Germany in two weeks. – 11. He/She said he/she **had been** playing football. – 12. He/She said she/the girl **was** Elke and that she **came** from Dortmund, too. He/She said she/Elke **had come** to the park after she had **done** her homework.

4

1. a) She said (that) she **was** staying **here tonight**.
   b) She told me yesterday morning she **was** staying **here for the night/on Sunday night**.
   c) On Sunday she informed me that she **was** staying **there/in Leeds for the night/on Sunday night**.
2. a) Peter told me that he **had seen** John **here on Monday/the day before yesterday**.
   b) Peter told me that he **had seen** John **in London on Monday**.
   c) Peter rang me and said that he **had seen** John **here yesterday**.
3. a) A friend recommended me to come **to Ireland** for my holiday **this year**.
   b) John advised me to go **to Ireland** for my holiday **next year**.
   c) I was advised to go **to Ireland** for my holiday **last year**.

5

1. Our teacher told us (that) he **had** to go and see the headmaster, **so** he asked us **to take** out our books and do the exercise on page 23. *or:* Our teacher asked us **to take** out our books … **because** he **had** to go and see the headmaster. – 2. My mother asked me **to give** her my old jeans **because** she **wanted** to wash them. – 3. My brother told me/said he **had lent** me £2 and asked me **to give** it him back. –

4. My sister told me **to take** that/the T-shirt off because it **was** hers. — 5. My friend asked me **to have** another biscuit and told me/**because** he **had** got plenty. — 6. The/A policeman told/warned us that the/this road **had been flooded** and asked us **to follow** the DIVERSION signs. — 7. My uncle asked me **to come** in and **sit** down. Then he asked me **to have** a cup of tea and said/told me that/**because** he **hadn't been** expecting me so early. — 8. The inspector told me that the/this ticket **was** only valid with a Young Person's Railcard, **so** he asked me to show him my Railcard. — 9. My/Her ex-boyfriend told me/her **to go** home **because** he **hadn't invited** me/her to his party. — 10. The notice advised us **to avoid** the last-minute rush and **to post** early for Christmas. *or:* ...to avoid the last-minute rush **by posting** early for Christmas.

6

a) 1. I want to know if this exercise is difficult./... if the water is warm enough for swimming. — 2. She wanted to find out whether she could get a bus to Chelsham. — 3. He asked me if I knew the right answer. — 4. Our teacher sometimes asks if we do our homework on the bus. — 5. The man asked her whether she had seen his umbrella. — 6. My mother wants to know if this exercise is difficult./... if you'll be staying for supper. — 7. The driver inquired whether the hotel had a good garage. — 8. He wondered if his parents knew where he was. — 9. They wanted to know if their son had received their letter yet. — 10. I wonder whether the water is warm enough for swimming.

b) 1. "Is this exercise difficult?" / "Is the water warm enough for swimming?" — 2. "Can I get a bus to Chelsham?" — 3. "Do you know the right answer?" — 4. "Do you do your homework on the bus?" — 5. "Have you seen my umbrella?" — 6. "Is this exercise difficult?" / "Will he/she/your friend be staying for supper?" — 7. "Does the hotel have/Has the hotel got a good garage?" — 8. "Do my parents know where I am?" — 9. "Has our son/Have you received our letter yet?" — 10. "Is the water warm enough for swimming?"

7

1. My father asked me who **had left** the front door open. — 2. She wants to know what (on earth) we **are doing** here. — 3. His friend asked her how much money she **had (got)**. — 4. The reporter requested information about how many prisoners **had escaped** before the prison staff **had found** the hole. — 5. He wants to know when the football match **took** place. — 6. The motorist asked the mechanic how soon he **could** repair his car. — 7. Our youth leader wanted to know what **had happened** to John. — 8. One of the tourists has just asked me how far Reading **is** from London. — 9. The child asked his mother where flies **went** in the winter. — 10. The detective asked me what I **had done** after I **had left** the hotel.

8

1. The sergeant **ordered** the soldier **to wake up, and asked/asking him** what **was** the matter with him.
2. Ken **said** he **loved** French wine, and **asked** Peter **to pass him** the bottle.
3. Peter **asked if/whether** Patrick **liked** wine, too, and **suggested that they should offer/suggested offering** him some.
4. The wife **told** her husband to pay attention **to her and said that she had to** tell him everything twice.
5. Tania **ordered/commanded** her dog Robin **to come to her, asked/asking him** where **he had got** those sausages and **said/saying that he was** a bad dog.
6. The manager of the firm **asked** the young lady **if she was** Janet Smith. **When she said she was, he asked her to come** in and **sit** down. **Then he offered her** a cigarette/**asked her if she wanted** a cigarette.
7. Angela **told** her boyfriend Derek **that she had been** surprised not to see **him** at Phil's party. **She asked him** where **he had been the previous night, warning him/ and warned him to tell her** the truth.
8. Oliver **suggested that we should wait/suggested waiting** a few minutes longer. **He told me he had** no idea where the others **had** got to, **and asked me whether I thought** they **were** lost.
9. The driving instructor **told** my sister/brother **to stop, said/saying he/she had run** over a hen **and asked/asking why he/she couldn't drive** more carefully.
10. My teacher **suggested that we should finish/suggested finishing** this exercise and **have/having** a break. **I said that was** a good idea.

9

1. *Reporter:* When **did** you **start** to take ecstasy?
   Sarah: It **was** at a party.
   Reporter: What **made** you start?
   Sarah: Everyone else at the party **was taking** something. I **felt** a bit of an outsider.
   Reporter: **Have** you ever **tried** any other drugs?
   Sarah: A friend **offered** me a joint last week, but I **refused** it.
   Reporter: **Do** you **think** you **will want** to try stronger drugs now?
   Sarah: No. Ecstasy **gives** me all I need.
2. *Reporter:* How long **have** you **been selling** drugs, Darrel?
   Darrel: I **started** while I **was** still at school. I**'ve been selling** ecstasy and other tablets for about three years now.
   Reporter: **Don't** you **have** a bad conscience about exploiting young people?
   Darrel: No. I **know** that the tablets I**'m selling are** good quality stuff.
   Reporter: **How much do** these tablets **cost**?

Darrel:	That **depends** on what each customer **wants**.
Reporter:	**What do** you **mean**?
Darrel:	Some of the kids **like** to mix ecstasy with LSD and cocaine.
Reporter:	**Don't** you **think** taking cocaine **is** the way into the hard drugs scene?
Darrel:	Perhaps it **is**. It**'s** a risk the kids **have** to take.
3. *Reporter:*	**How did** your daughter **get** involved in drugs?
Mrs Tate:	Sheila **began** with dance drugs like ecstasy.
Reporter:	**How** old **was** she when she **started**?
Mrs Tate:	Sheila **was** only fourteen. My husband and I **were** horrified when she **was brought** home early one morning in an ambulance.
Reporter:	**Weren't** you **able to/Couldn't** you **stop** her? She was only fourteen, after all.
Mrs Tate:	We **tried**, but the attraction of drugs **was** stronger. All her friends **were** on drugs.
Reporter:	**What happened** after that?
Mrs Tate:	She **went** from ecstasy and LSD to cocaine and heroin. She**'s having** medical treatment at a drugs centre at the moment. Sheila's addiction **broke** up our marriage. My ex-husband still **blames** me for what **(has) happened** to our only child.

Test

Bei den unterstrichenen Wörtern mussten Zeit- oder Ortsverschiebungen vorgenommen werden.

1. "Put your hands up and don't move or we'll shoot!
2. Nobody will get hurt if you do what you are told."
3. "Where do you keep the keys to the safe?"
4. "There is no money in the safe. It has already been collected.
5. A security van came at 9 o'clock <u>this</u> morning."
6. The bank robber told him not to lie to them. He said they had been watching the bank all morning.
7. The manager insisted that it was the truth and (said/told him) that the van had come to the back door of the bank.
8. The robber said/told him that he didn't believe him and ordered him to open the safe anyway.
9. He warned the manager / The robber said that if he/the manager didn't open the safe, they would shoot him.
10. The manager told him/dared him to go ahead and asked him if he knew that the police were on their way <u>there/to the bank</u>. He said he could hear their sirens at <u>that</u> very moment!

Partizipien – Gerundium – Infinitiv 9

1

1. interested in; very interesting — 2. frightening experience; frightened of — 3. boiling water; hard-boiled eggs — 4. falling rain; fallen leaves — 5. fully booked; booking-office — 6. be terrified of; nothing terrifying about — 7. worn out

2

many people **living** in London — Cockney was the dialect **spoken** by people **born** in the East End — the church bells of St Mary-le-Bow (**known** as Bow Bells) — Foreigners **listening** to a real Cockney — A Cockney **saying**: … — Cockneys **educated** at grammar schools — someone less well **educated**

3

1. The man **standing** — 2. The one **wearing** — 3. The one **dressed** — 4. the man **wanted** by — 5. the man **living** in — 6. that bank **situated** — 7. the one **invited** to — 8. one of the men **working** at — 9. a Scottish name **beginning** with Mac — 10. that chain of restaurants **selling**

4

2. The money **lying/found** in the suitcase was stolen from Lloyds Bank. *or:* The money **stolen** from Lloyds Bank was found in a suitcase. — 3. The girl **sitting** on the bench is reading a book. *or:* The girl **reading** a book is sitting on a bench. — 4. The letter **posted** on 12 August is lying on the desk. *or:* The letter **lying** on the desk was posted on 12 August. — 5. The car **parked** in front of the house is from Britain. *or:* The car **registered** in Britain is/was parked in front of the house. — 6. The languages **spoken** here are English, French and German. — 7. The Queen is the woman **going** shopping at Harrods/into the store. *or:* The woman **going** shopping at Harrods/into the store is the Queen. — 8. The woman **being interviewed** here is the actress Jane Jones. *or:* The actress Jane Jones is the woman **being interviewed** here. — 9. "Hamlet" is the play **being put on/performed** at this theatre. *or:* The play **being put on/performed** at this theatre is "Hamlet".

5

1. **Walking** across the room, I shut the door. — 2. **Having listened** to the new CD, we went out for a hamburger. — 3. **Not knowing** the way, he asked a passer-by. — 4. *No change.* — 5. Unless **taught** English properly, they will not be able to get good jobs abroad. — 6. **When leaving** the train, passengers should take all their luggage with them. — 7. Stay calm if **stopped** by a policeman. — 8. Though **made** in Korea, this car

is still very good. — 9. *No change.* — 10. **Walking** into the room, the headmaster sat down at the teacher's table. — 11. *No change. or:* She had no worries until **told to leave** the country within 48 hours. — 12. John went to Oxford after **getting/having got** four A's in his A-levels.

6

1. **Shutting** the door, he sat down. — 2. **Having passed** my driving test, I bought a car. — 3. She sat in the bath **reading** a newspaper. - **(While) Sitting** in the bath she read a newspaper. — 4. **Not wanting** to go, we stayed at home. — 5. **Not having learnt** French at school, I wasn't able to read the letter. — 6. My friend fell asleep **(while) watching** TV. — 7. **Not living** in the area, she could not help me. — 8. Our dog ran off, **having bitten** the postman. *or:* **Having bitten** the postman, our dog ran off. — 9. **Being** foreigners, they had to learn English. — 10. **Walking** to school, I learn ten English words on the way. *or:* I walk to school **learning** ten English words on the way.

7

1. She just sat there **watching** TV. — 2. The children went **running** down to the beach. — 3. The policemen just stood there **waiting** for orders. — 4. The food remained **untouched.** — 5. He spends a lot of time **dancing** in discos. — 6. The farmer caught two campers **camping** in his field without permission. — 7. They have wasted a lot of time **playing** football at the weekends. — 8. The sailor lay on the grass **drunk**. *or:* The sailor lay **drunk** on the grass. — 9. They spent a lot of time **sunbathing**. — 10. I can't stand here all day **waiting** for you! *or:* I can't stand here **waiting** for you all day!

8

1. I saw/watched several people **waiting** for the bus.
   I saw/watched a street musician **playing** in the Underground.
   I saw/watched several people **looking** at the shop windows.
2. I watched the traffic **driving** up and down.
3. I listened to a street musician **playing** in the Underground.
   I listened to a police siren **wailing** in the distance.
4. I heard several people **speaking** German.
   I heard a police siren **wailing** in the distance.
   I heard a jet plane **break** the sound barrier.
5. I felt the hot sun **warming** the back of my neck.
   I felt a hand **touch** my shoulder. It was my good friend Bob …

9

Gerund:
I like living in the big city. — Working as an archaeologist must be fun. — I wouldn't mind studying archaeology — I love walking around the streets of London — streets which you can only reach by walking through narrow alleys — I have got used to hearing the sound of traffic — but living near the centre of a town — I must stop writing now and start doing my homework. — I look forward to seeing you at Christmas.

Present participle:
London is a living museum! — Sitting on the upper deck of a bus — the high wooden fence surrounding a big building site. — As well as building workers — students looking for Roman remains — The mist rising from the lakes — I would find myself writing about a big city — But after living in London for nearly four weeks — the sound of traffic rolling through the city — Waking up at night — makes life so much more interesting

Progressive form:
I've been living in Central London

10

1. Swimming is one of my hobbies. — 2. I like swimming in the sea. — 3. I soon got used to swimming in salt water. — 4. Swimming at the swimming baths is not as nice. — 5. I don't mind going to the/an open-air swimming pool at the weekend(s). — 6. My brother doesn't mind me/my going without him. — 7. Collecting old records/LPs is his favourite hobby. — 8. He finances/pays for his hobby by delivering newspapers. — 9. My mother doesn't like him/his having to deliver newspapers in bad weather. — 10. She is looking forward to him/his starting a proper job soon.

11

1. to remember; living — 2. moving — 3. to ask — 4. shopping — 5. finding — 6. asking — 7. to talk — 8. talking; telling — 9. leaving — 10. to live — 11. to mention — 12. to say

Test

1

1. My elder sister is a big, beefy 19-year old. She has always been interested in sport. — 2. When she was at school she played hockey in the school team. Playing hockey was one of her hobbies. — 3. They even played in the middle of winter, when the ground was frozen! — 4. I went into her bedroom one day and saw a magazine lying on the floor. — 5. Picking it up, I saw that it was a paragliding magazine. — 6. "Hey, Sis!" I said in surprise. "You aren't thinking of learning to paraglide, are you?" — 7. "Why not?" she replied. "It's a great hobby. You spend all your time reading books!" — 8. "But what will Mum and Dad say? They won't want to see you break an arm or a leg - or your neck!" — 9. Just then we heard the front door open. — 10. It was our parents coming back from shopping. My sister looked angrily at me and said: "If you tell Mum and Dad anything about this, I'll break your neck!"

2

1c), 2c), 3b), 4b), 5c), 6a), 7c), 8a), 9b), 10b)

Das Passiv 10

1

1. we will be met at the airport. — 2. are opened. — 3. rooms were booked — 4. can be taken — 5. are made on Malta. — 6. were picked up — 7. are visited — 8. A coach trip can be taken — 9. may/can not be booked — 10. has been arranged

2

1. is understood — 2. is real English spoken? — 3. tourists are disliked — 4. was stolen — 5. has been cleaned — 6. hadn't been made — 7. I am/we are liked

3

1. A heavily-armed police riot squad broke up a peaceful demonstration in Trafalgar Square yesterday.-- 2. Angry policemen arrested several (peaceful) demonstrators. — 3. After the riot squad had been called, probably by unnamed police informers, — 4. armour-plated police Land Rovers brought about twenty policemen in riot gear to Trafalgar Square. — 5. Bullying constables ordered Jessica Davies, the leader of the demonstration, to ask her fellow demonstrators to go home. — 6. Angry police armed with heavy sticks took one or two demonstrators to Marlborough Street police station. Police kept them there overnight because they refused to give their names. — 7. Ms Catherine Binyon, chairperson of PEACE NOW, has not yet been released. — 8. During the past few months our peaceful organization has held four demonstrations.

4

1. Industrial waste is being discharged into the river. — 2. Rubbish is being dumped in the woods/forests. — 3. Private cars are not being used efficiently. — 4. Valuable raw materials are being thrown away. — 5. Public transport is not being used enough — 6. A new hypermarket with a huge car park is being built. — 7. Railway stations are being closed./This railway station is being closed on 1st August. — 8. Gas-guzzlers are still being developed. — 9. Old paper and cardboard boxes are not being recycled. --10. Cigarette advertising is (still) not being banned.

5

"Nothing is being done about air pollution (by the present Government). Two new by-passes and another twenty miles of motorway are being built in my constituency alone! Last year they promised to halt construction of a nuclear power station which was being planned, but nothing has been done, and land near the River Don is already being surveyed in preparation for construction of this power station which is not wanted! The rivers in this beautiful part of Britain are still being polluted. Last year chemicals factories were still being expanded even though an enquiry into chemical pollution had been promised!"

6

Einige Lösungsvorschläge:

1. This book was written by a famous author/an Englishman.
2. Thatched houses are not built in Britain any longer.
3. Live music is often played/is being played here/in this pub/was being played here last week.
4. Good sandwiches are made/sold in this snack bar.
5. Excellent fruit is grown by these farmers/on this farm.
6. Gas-guzzlers are/were still being built/made by some car companies/are still not banned by the government.
7. The environment is still being polluted with chemicals/by some big firms.
8. Young people are (being) trained as doctors.
9. Many souvenirs are made/sold here every year.
10. Spanish is spoken in Spain/many countries of South and Central America.

7

1. More industrial waste is being dumped in our rivers than ever before — 2. Prince William was being followed by 10 photographers yesterday — 3. The Nobel peace prize has been awarded to a dog! — 4. A famous film star is being divorced by her fifth husband — 5. Good marks have been "sold" to pupils (by a teacher) for years — 6. Foreign aid money was being spent on arms — 7. Drugs were taken by champion runner — 8. Traffic in northern Scotland is being stopped by 3 metres of snow — 9. Baby seals have been killed again (by hunters) — 10. Pop star Madonna's next concert will be cancelled — 11. A dog is bitten by a man — 12. Many parts of Britain are being flooded (by heavy rain)

8

1. Plenty is being done! — 2. The problem is being looked into at this very moment! — 3. I don't care what is being worked out by your cousin's firm — 4. A traffic-free zone will/is going to be set up as soon as — 5. More people are knocked down and injured — 6. who would be locked up! — 7. You mean this matter has been/was talked about at a meeting — 8. the matter was brought up at the end of the meeting — 9. I think the pavements are being obstructed by all those cars! — 10. It's not a bigger car park that is needed — 11. Bikes can't be towed away! — 12. But bikes have to be chained up! ... Thirty bikes have been stolen already this year!

9

1. **I was handed** the note. — 2. **I have** never **been offered** a ride in her car! — 3. **Weren't you sent** an invitation to his party? — 4. **Haven't you been taught** to say "please" if you want something? — 5. **You won't be told** the truth. — 6. **We are being denied** our basic rights! — 7. **I was being given** an injection when the lights went out. — 8. **She is going to be awarded** first prize in the photographic competition. — 9. **I haven't been shown** the photos yet. — 10. **This bike wasn't stolen. It was sold** to me. — 11. **She was promised** a new skateboard for Christmas. — 12. **I have been left** £5,000 by my great-grandfather/in my great-grandfather's will.

10

1. This parcel **was delivered** to the wrong address. — 2. This problem **can't be explained** to people who know nothing about cricket. — 3. They **have not been introduced** to the President yet. — 4. The scenery **can** only **be described** to you with the help of these photos. — 5. The following solution **is proposed** to you. — 6. After the experiment **had been demonstrated** (to the pupils), the laboratory was full of smoke. — 7. The results of the elections **were announced** to the angry crowd. — 8. Nothing **was said** about this to me. — 9. Clothes **are being distributed** to the refugees. — 10. An alternative **was suggested** to the worried workers.

11

1. We **had been told** that our bank was robbery-proof. — 2. The alarm system **was said to be** perfect. … — 3. The bank's security arrangements **are** now **felt to have been** inadequate. — 4. The robbers **are believed to have been hiding** in the bank all night. We **were surprised** when we arrived for work. — 5. We **were told to put up** our hands. — 6. Then we **were made to lie** down on the floor. — 7. The gang **is supposed to be** the same one that robbed the National Westminster Bank in Croydon last month. — 8. These men **are known to be** dangerous criminals! — 9. We **were told** not to move for ten minutes — 10. because other crooks **were said to be** outside, watching in case the alarm **was given**. — 11. The robbers **were seen to leave** (the bank) in a fast car. — 12. When they had gone the manager, Mr Simms, **was found to have had** a mild heart-attack!

Test

1. *correct*
2. The company **was founded** in the 1920s.
3. The first cars which **were produced** were cheap three-wheelers.
4. *correct*
5. One of the original three-wheelers **was** recently **sold** for £25,000!
6. Many of these old cars **have been driven** for hundreds of thousands of miles!
7. *correct*
8. Until recently, buyers **were invited** to come to the factory at any time to see their cars while they **were being built**.
9. But that tradition **was thought** to hold up production. So it **was stopped**.
10. In future, buyers **will be asked** to make an appointment before visiting the factory.

Modale Hilfsverben

1

List One - Modal auxiliaries:

This Evacuation Order **must** be observed — (persons) **should** apply to the Commanding Officer — who **may** be able to help. — Residents **must** take all their furniture — No exceptions **can** be made — The general public **may** only visit — people **must not** leave the roads — because they **might** be injured — that the Army **ought to** keep its promise and **should** return Imber to the people

List Two - Substitutes:

Imber **is to be** evacuated on 1st December 1943. — Any persons who **are not able to** find accommodation — no one **will be allowed to** return — Residents **will be able to** return — the last 150 residents … **had to** leave their homes — They **were allowed to** take their possessions — but **were forbidden** (= not allowed) to return to the village — only St Giles Church … and a few buildings **have been allowed** to remain

List Three - Other tense-forming auxiliaries:

NOTICE **is** hereby given … — From 2nd December 1943, all roads … **will** be CLOSED … — No exceptions **can** be made to this Order, which **is** issued in the interests of National Security. — They … **were** forbidden to return to the village.

2

1. Do we have — 2. needn't — 3. mustn't — 4. had; I'll/will have — 5. has/will have/is having — 6. We've/have had — 7. Why have you had — 8. needn't — 9. must

3

1. will be able to — 2. has never had — 3. were able — 4. have never been able — 5. to be able to — 6. will have to — 7. to be able to — 8. would be able — 9. hadn't been able to — 10. can't/haven't been able to — 11. will have to

4

1. be allowed to — 2. be allowed to — 3. may not — 4. may not — 5. was allowed to — 6. may — 7. we'll be allowed to — 8. Were you allowed to — 9. weren't allowed to — 10. May — 11. Might — 12. might — 13. may — 14. might — 15. may/might

5

1. "**May** I borrow your book?" — 2. "**Might** I possibly use your/your father's computer?" — 3. "I think this £5 note **may** be a forgery." — 4. "I think you **might** be too young to watch the horror video with me." — 5. "We **may** take/have a holiday in Spain next

year." — 6. "If we had more money we **might** take/have a holiday on Hawaii." — 7. "You **may** not borrow my Rolls Royce!" — 8. "I don't think we **will be allowed to** go alone." — 9. "If my brother went with us I think I **would be allowed to** go to the pop concert in Edinburgh next week." — 10. "You **may** be right." — 11. "It **might** be right/wrong." — 12. "At home I**'ve** always **been allowed to** watch my favourite programme (on TV)!"

6

1. "**Shall we go** for a bike-ride in the country?" — 2. "Perhaps we **should take** our rain capes with us." — 3. "Perhaps we **oughtn't to/shouldn't go** too far." — 4. "The little lake on the edge of the forest **is said to be good for swimming**." — 5. "Hey! You **oughtn't to/shouldn't cycle** on the left-hand side in Germany!" — 6. "I **ought to know** that by now!" — 7. "It**'s supposed/said to be** haunted." — 8. "**Shall we have** a look around?" — 9. "That sign means nobody **is supposed** to go inside the house." — 10. "Perhaps we **oughtn't to/shouldn't**/we**'d better not go** in, then." — 11. "Yes, if **anyone/someone were to see** us we might get into trouble." — 12. "I think we **should/ought to**/we**'d better go** home before it gets dark."

7

1. "**Do** you **wish/want to** speak to me, Headmaster? — 2. "Oh, Karin! Yes. I **was going/ wanted/ intended to** phone you this morning." — 3. "Why?" - "I **was going to/wanted to** ask you if you would like to take part in our Class Excursion/Trip." — 4. "I really **intended/meant to** stay at home at the weekend. — 5. My aunt **wants/is going/ intends/(means) to** visit us." — 6. They **wanted/intended to** see the film, but did not **want/intend to** queue for tickets. — 7. "What **do you intend/are you going to** do with the money?" — 8. "I**'m going to** buy a mountain bike. — 9. I**'ve** always **wanted to** have a mountain bike."

Test

1. "Is it really necessary? **Must** we go to the school concert tonight?
2. "If you don't want to go, you **needn't**."
3. "But I can see you think that we both **ought** to go, don't you?"
4. "I **could** *(can – nicht so gut geeignet)* go alone if you're too busy."
5. "Well, perhaps we **shouldn't have** bought two tickets if you're so busy."
6. You **must** arrive on time.
7. **Can/May** I talk to him now?
8. **Might** I possibly ask you a very personal question?
9. We **should** really stop here for the night.
10. She **would** watch TV until bedtime every night.

Relativsätze

12

1

Lösungsvorschläge:

1. A toaster is a device **which/that is used / you use for making toast**.
2. A winner is a person **who/that wins a prize, a race, etc**.
3. Dinner is a meal **which/that you eat / is eaten in the evening**.
4. A fridge is a device **which/that keeps food cool /which you find in most kitchens**.
5. A bike is a device **which/that you use to get to school on time**.
6. A manager is a person **who/that manages/runs a shop/company/business**.
7. A wristwatch is a (kind of) small clock **which/that you wear on your wrist**.
8. Soap is a thing/something **which/that you use when you wash / to wash with**.
9. Jam is a food **which/that you put on bread and butter / which you eat for breakfast**.
10. Commas are things/punctuation marks **which/that separate a main and subordinate clause** in German/that German grammar is very fond of.

2

1. I saw the Harry Potter films first. Then Mum bought me all the books, **which were very expensive**.
2. He only bought cheap paperbacks. He didn't buy books **that/which were very expensive**.
3. I have two sisters. This is a photo of my sister **who/that is 16 years old**.
4. My friend Harold, **who is 16 years old,** lives in Bournemouth.
5. The woman **who/that teaches us** French is OK,
6. but old Mr Strickland, **who teaches us** German, is very strict.
7. Mum drives the car **which/that is in the garage**.
8. My dad uses his old bike, **which is in the garage,** too.
9. "My girlfriend, **who has red hair,** lives next-door to me."
10. "There's a girl **who/that has red hair** in my class at school. She lives in your street, I think. Is she your girlfriend?"

3

Bei den Pronomen, die in Klammern stehen, handelt es sich um Relativpronomen, die in der Umgangssprache oft weggelassen werden – aus der direkten „pronomenlosen" Berührung zwischen Haupt- und Relativsatz entsteht der so genannte *contact clause*.

1. Have you heard the CD **(which/that)** I lent to your sister Caroline?

2. This is the boy **(who(m)/that)** I saw at the disco last week.
3. Here's my new bike, **which** I got for my birthday.
4. This is Linda**, who(m)** we talked to at Jim's party.
5. They are the new group **(which/that)** you heard on the radio yesterday evening. *(Hier wäre auch „(who/whom)" möglich, da es sich bei einer Gruppe natürlich auch um Personen handelt.)*
6. John didn't see the car **(which/that)** the bank-robbers escaped in.
7. We all know Mickey Mouse**, (who/whom)** Walt Disney invented.
8. I like milk chocolate**, which** you can buy all over the world.
9. Have you read Petra's e-mail**, which** she sent two days ago?
10. You're the man **(who/whom/that)** I've been waiting for since lunchtime.
11. This is my bike**, which** I left in the garden overnight.
12. He wrote to a Scottish girl **(who/whom/that)** he met in Spain last month.

4

Je nachdem, ob du annimmst, der *British way of life* sei in **allen** Commonwealth-Ländern kritiklos übernommen worden oder nur in **bestimmten** Ländern, brauchst du das Komma im ersten Satz. Dir ist sicher klar, warum!

Rugby is a game which/that is extremely popular in Britain, France, Australia, South Africa, New Zealand and in fact many other Commonwealth countries(,) in which the British way of life predominated. The game was 'invented' by a boy who was a pupil at Rugby School in 1823. He was the first player who ("that" ist hier zwar möglich, ist aber vor einem eingekapselten Nebensatz unüblich), during a normal game of football, in which players normally only kicked the ball, picked up the ball, which in those days was not perfectly round but slightly oval (as it still is in rugby and American football today), and ran with it.
There are two types of rugby: Rugby Union, which is an amateur sport played at schools, and Rugby League, a professional sport (which/that) many people watch every Saturday in the North of England. There are fifteen players in a Rugby Union team and only thirteen in a Rugby League team. International rugby matches, which the French and Welsh enjoy more than soccer matches, are played under Rugby Union rules and are well attended by thousands of fans, who often travel long distances to see the games.
The 'inventor' of the game, William Webb Ellis, who(m) few people know by name, became a clergyman in later life, and died in 1872

5

Three students meet in the Hall of Residence on the first day of term.

1. One of them is Kevin, **whose** friend Günter has just arrived from Germany.
2. Günter is the German exchange student **whose** parents invited Kevin to stay during the summer vacation.
3. Kevin's best friend John is standing in front of the notice board in the corridor, **whose** notices/**the notices of which** are usually very interesting.
4. Kevin introduces his two friends to each other. "This is John, **whose** parents are good friends of ours.
5. John, this is Günter, my German friend **whose** parents I stayed with during the summer vac."
6. "Hello, John. I'm the exchange student from Germany **whose** room is on the floor above yours."
7. "Pleased to meet you. Is that your car outside?" – "Which car?" – "The blue VW **whose** windows / **the windows of which** are all open."
8. "Did I leave the windows open? It was so hot in town! I was stuck in a traffic jam behind a long line of cars **whose** drivers/**the drivers of which** all seemed to be asleep!
9. Should I go downstairs and shut the windows? Are there many car thieves on the campus?" – "Last term thieves stole several cars **whose** owners/**the owners of which** had forgotten to lock them!"
10. "I'll go down and lock my car right away." But suddenly the three students heard a voice from a loudspeaker in the corridor: "Will the owner of the blue VW, German registration number HN-LS 317, **whose** windows are open and **whose** doors are unlocked/**the windows of which** are open and **the doors of which** are unlocked, please come downstairs at once." – "Oops!" said Günter, and ran off down the corridor.

6

An old country railway station **which** the Council wanted to pull down has been saved at the last minute. The "Save our Station" campaign**, whose** leader/**the leader of which** is Robin Wilson**,** talked to our reporter and said that experts had examined the part of the building **whose** walls / **the walls of which** the council had said were unsafe. The experts said that the walls only needed a few simple repairs**, which** any local builder could do. The money **which/that** had been given by supporters of the campaign/**(which/that)** supporters of the campaign had given was/would be almost enough for the repairs. Many people heard about the campaign**, which** was publicised by local radio stations. They criticised the Council**, whose** decision/ **the decision of which** was not widely publicised. Robin Wilson is now looking for volunteers **who/that** can come and help do the necessary repair work**, which** will take about four weeks. The chairman of the Council committee **who** *(„that" könnte hier heißen, dass das **Komitee** die Entscheidung gefällt hat: wenn die **Person** gemeint ist, sollte man „who" verwenden, um Verwechslungen zu vermeiden)* made the decision is very angry. Robin Williams**, who(m)** local people admire**,** got married last week. He met his wife**, who** comes from London**,** as a result of his campaign work. They are both dynamic people **who(m)/that** *(Weglassung hier aus Betonungsgründen nicht zu empfehlen)* the Council chairman dislikes intensely.

7

1. She said she couldn't help me**, which** was just an excuse.
2. He arrived half an hour late**, which** was very impolite of him.
3. My sister watches TV a lot**, which** is not good for her.
4. Last week I went to a family wedding**, which** I usually hate!
5. All my cousins were there**, which** made the wedding more fun.
6. Even my great-grandmother was there**, which** astonished everyone.
7. The old lady is 99 years old**, which** makes her the oldest member of our family.
8. When my father saw my last school report, he got very angry**, which** didn't surprise me.
9. I had bad marks in most subjects**, which** I couldn't explain.
10. Luckily I had a 2 for English**, which** surprised my father.
11. He told me his best mark for English at school had been a 3**, which** shocked me.
12. His marks in other subjects had been bad too**, which** I didn't know!

8

1. This is the book which I was telling you about. I read it in three days**,** which is very fast for me! It's a story about a pop group which started up at our school.

2. Tom suggested a party**,** which I thought was a good idea. Then Jenny suggested a barbecue**,** which sounded like an even better idea. She said she had plenty of charcoal left from the barbecue which they had had last week.
3. He said he played the guitar in a pop group which was very good. His sister said that she was a singer in the same group**,** which is nonsense. My friend John told me it was a true story**,** which I didn't believe. But he has often told me stories which I didn't believe.

9

1. I find it hard to believe **what he tells me**.
2. **What** is important is to learn ten new words a day.
3. Tell me something about **what your mother does**.
4. **What he did** was hard to explain.
5. I watched him carefully but couldn't observe **what he did** exactly.
6. **What they suggested** was out of the question.
7. Three strong men are **what is needed** to move this piano.
8. A big portion of fish and chips is precisely **what I want/wish**.
9. **What you think** is not important. **What you do** is.
10. **What** goes on at my school would surprise you!
11. "I've no idea **what he thinks**." – "**What he thinks** doesn't interest me! It's **what he does** that matters!"

Test

1. I read the book **(which/that)** you lent me.
2. It was the noise of the traffic which kept her awake.
3. He asked me a question that I couldn't answer.
4. He asked me a personal question, **which** was very rude of him.
5. She is good at English**, which** will help her in her new job.
6. We watched the rest of the match **whose** first half (*heute weniger gebräuchlich:* the first half **of which**) we had missed.
7. Mike Summers**,** about **whom** I told you/**who** I told you about**,** lives next door to us.
8. The friend from **whom** I got this letter / **(who)** I got this letter from lives in Germany.
9. "Me? Angry? I don't know **what** you mean! I'm not angry!"
10. He suggested going swimming, **which** I thought was a good idea.
11. **What** he said is probably true.
12. The Mr Brown **who** lives in our street is no relation to your Mr Brown.

Stressfreies Lernen und bessere Noten mit dem Aktiv-Lernprogramm

Mit **Mein Erfolgstrainer** kannst du dir dein individuelles Lernprogramm zusammenstellen. Die Einteilung des Stoffes in **Lerneinheiten mit Zeitplanung** hilft dir dabei.

Aufgaben mit Regeln und Anwendungsbeispielen erleichtern dir das selbstständige Üben zu Hause. **Ausführliche Lösungen** garantieren dir eine gute Vorbereitung auf **Klassenarbeiten und Prüfungen.**

Mein Erfolgstrainer
Rechtschreibung
9./10. Schuljahr
ISBN 978-3-12-927135-3
Preis: 13,95 €

Mein Erfolgstrainer
Aufsatz
7. – 10. Schuljahr
ISBN 978-3-12-927196-4
Preis: 13,95 €

Diese und weitere Klett-Lernhilfen sind im Buchhandel erhältlich.

Informationen finden Sie unter **www.klett.de/lernhilfen**